◀Pwning N00bs▶

Or

(Owning Newbs)

The PC Gamer's Guide

to

Hardware, Strategy, and Tactics

By John David

johndavidauthor.com

Available online in ebook, paperback, and audiobook (v.62012)

◀TABLE OF CONTENTS▶

◄INTRODUCTION►

"Pwning N00bs" (pronounced *owning noobs*) is a gaming term used to describe the utter domination of a player or players by another, or by several others, as is usually the case. A "noob" (also "newb," "nub" and "n00b") is of course a new player, perhaps new to a particular game, or new to gaming in general. All gamers have been noobs at one point or another, and I always feel like one every time I open up a fresh game and set foot upon an unfamiliar virtual battleground for the first time.

All games have a "learning curve." Some are steeper than others. Your goal is to flatten out that curve as quickly as possible, and reduce the amount of "pwning" you are subjected to. *Pwning N00bs* will help you do that by giving you the benefit of my 12 years of hard-won experience with online, or "MMORPG" type PC games. That experience is mostly limited to combat-type simulations, of all different kinds.

Although I have never been a "leet" (elite) player in any of them, to the extent that I could be considered a "world-class" gamer, I was and am very proficient at all the games that I have put in the effort to master. Games such as *MechWarrior*, the *Battlefield* series, and of course *Left for Dead*. On any given day, on any given server, I can be found among the high-scoring players, usually the top five.

Games succeed or fail based on the devotion of their players and fans. Titles that are too complex, or too difficult to understand and master never become "hits," and therefore usually quietly fade away into obscurity. Others, like *MechWarrior*, become cult favorites, and seem to go on forever in one incarnation or another. This guide is not about those games, or about any particular game, specifically. Instead, this book is a "general" guide to acquiring the "tools" for success in the genre of PC gaming itself.

All successful games (and gamers) share many common characteristics. "Hit" games are easy to understand, and offer a degree of complexity that is deep enough to prevent boredom, but simple enough to make playing them fun. They also offer a control scheme that is customizable, so that each player can configure their own hardware setup according to their particular playing style, and the limitations of that hardware.

Successful gamers are patient, eager to learn, observant, and have properly configured and optimized their hardware. Some players will blame "hardware" deficiencies for their lack of success or skill, but usually better hardware is not the "Holy Grail" of gaming proficiency that many claim it to be. However, just as building a house will require at least a hammer and some nails, you will need some basic tools to develop your proficiency as a PC gamer.

For example, I started playing *MechWarrior* on my very first home PC, an *emachines* of all things, with "onboard" graphics and sound, very little memory, and abysmal processing speed. Within a few weeks, I was recruited to join a "Clan," mostly because of my noobish enthusiasm, and certainly not because of my intimidating hardware. This taught me the first of many important gaming lessons, especially for combat simulations:

▪Skill can overcome the lack of good hardware, but good hardware seldom if ever overcomes the lack of skill▪

My first gaming name or "handle" was "Guts4Glory," and I chose that name because that was my combat strategy—find the enemy, charge in with all guns blazing, destroy or be destroyed, then wash, rinse, and repeat. I figured that the worst thing that could happen was I would "die," and then get a new "mech," (basically a giant walking tank) for free!

This is your basic noob strategy, and it is found on many servers, for many games, across the entire gaming universe.

It is called "noob rushing," and if you do it often, your teammates may say some unkind things to you, because teamwork is important to "winning," and your insistence on wasting assets, lives, and resources will not make you many friends. Ironically, some gamers are *very* serious about having fun, and are extremely intolerant of noobs and their behavior. They are also not shy about telling you so, or even "kicking" and "banning" you.

One day I was enacting my standard plan of charging in, *banzai* style, when I found myself in a small valley behind a hill, on one of my favorite maps. In the valley were three enemy mechs, including the "best" (top-scoring) player in the round, the leader of a Clan, known for his tactics of staying just out of the range of most weapons, and then blasting noobs into oblivion with long-range missiles. *MechWarrior* allowed you to customize your weapons platforms, and I tended to use short-range, ballistic-type weapons with fast reload times, and very little heat buildup.

The short story is that in about 60 seconds, only one mech was left standing in that valley—mine. I was as surprised as those three members of the other team must have been, (probably more so!) but really, all the factors needed for gaming success merely came together for me, in the same place, at the same time. The right strategy, in this case, surprise and speed, the right weapons, fast-loading, low heat, and a whole boatload of just plain beginner's luck all combined to make me look like I had been gaming for years.

▪The point here is that it is possible to game well, have fun, and almost never be on the bad side of an "pwning," if you remember a few simple universal gaming concepts and strategies▪

This guide will help you bring your hardware and skill level "up to speed" in a few hours, rather than in days or weeks, thereby saving you much embarrassment, grief, and *money*. It is intended for entry to mid-level gamers with stock systems and limited budgets.

Therefore, *Pwning N00bs* is not meant to be the "ultimate" gamer's guide, by any means, but if you study it carefully, you will become a much happier and more successful gamer, regardless of what game or games you play.

This guide is not intended to be a "build your own gaming PC from scratch" book, either.

▪Rather, the focus in the *Hardware* chapter will be on the *economical* optimization of the system you already have, versus the construction of an expensive new monster gaming rig▪

However, if you follow the concepts and directions given there, you will ultimately be able to do just that, if you have the time, energy, and budget. Working on your PC is interesting, easy, fun, and very safe if you are careful. Most PCs are built with "Plug and Play" modular components, and upgrading your system is typically no more complicated than "Out with the old, in with the new."

Usually you will not even need directions, but if you do, there are online tutorials for every component inside your case. Simply search "replace (your component) PC." If you can change a light bulb, you can change your video card, memory sticks, and sound card. If you can vacuum your car, you can clean dust out of your PC. If you can set up your home theater, you can do the same for your gaming entertainment system. So relax, have fun, and don't be afraid of your system or any individual component. They are just parts in a machine—there is nothing mystical, magical, or irreplaceable about them.

▪A very happy side-effect of having a PC that is optimized for gaming is that it will be much more efficient at other applications as well▪

Most of your non-gaming programs will open quicker and run faster, for example. If you do any video or sound editing and rendering, you will find that your system will burn discs and files without slowing down, even while you are multi-tasking elsewhere. You will especially notice this when using machines not your own, like your work or backup PC.

To help you get the most out of *Pwning N00bs*, this guide is arranged by chapter, beginning with a discussion of basic *Hardware* optimization and *Settings* configurations. With that said, I am not an engineer or scientist, and therefore any technical explanations that I provide will necessarily be in layman's terms, and are over-simplified as much as possible. This was done deliberately, to ensure that this guide is very easy to understand and use.

Strategies and Tactics is next, and finally the *Afterword* and *Key Concepts* sections. Throughout the text, many technical terms will be referenced back to the appropriate area of the guide that explains the particular item or concept. If you already have your PC hardware configured exactly as you want it, or are unable to perform any upgrades at this time, you may want to skip directly to the *Strategies and Tactics* chapter. However, I suggest that you read the section on *Settings* before you do, to ensure that you have not missed any useful tips or tweaks in your current setup.

Again, I have never been exclusively a gamer, with an unlimited budget of both time and money, playing for 16 hours a day in Mom's basement. <u>If that is you, most likely there will be little here that you will find unfamiliar</u>. But if you are like me, a casual gamer who likes to jump on a server once in a while for some fun and stress relief, without getting "pwned," then *Pwning N00bs* is the guide for you.

Enjoy!

▪DISCLAIMER▪

The material contained in this guide is for informational purposes only, and is *not* a recommendation of any particular course of action. By reading beyond this introduction, you accept and acknowledge that the decisions you make regarding your gaming experiences and hardware modifications remain your own, and not those of the author or publisher. If you disagree with this disclaimer, please stop reading now.

▪DISCLOSURE▪

Due to the large number of browser-based hyperlinks within the *ebook* text, you may wish to also purchase and use this guide on your PC or other web-enabled device. **External links and references to vendors and other information are provided for your convenience, are not guaranteed to work, and do not represent an endorsement by the author of any company, product, or service.** Neither the author nor publisher was compensated for the inclusion or exclusion of any link, product or website.

◀HARDWARE▶

All successful games are found on one or both of two platforms—console and PC. Each has advantages and disadvantages. Some games are only available on one or the other, so if you are a fan of a particular game, or you would like to be, you may find yourself by default setting up your gaming platform accordingly.

I am, and probably always will be, a devotee of the PC platform, originally because they were much more powerful and faster. They also offered greater customization options, better graphics and sound, plus the ability to interface via keyboard and mouse, versus the ubiquitous "controller." Like consoles, some PC games use specialized game controllers, in addition to the keyboard and mouse, such as joysticks, steering wheels, and the like.

Additionally, at the time I began to game, if you wanted "multiplayer" capability, that is, the ability to game against other human beings, versus the "Artificial Intelligence" or AI of the game, there simply were no options to do so outside of the PC environment. All that has changed now, of course, as console platforms and games have evolved so far that their hardware limitations are no longer as great a concern.

There are a few gamers who are very proficient at both the console and PC platforms, but typically you will find a "great divide" between the two.

Today, with the advent of high-definition television and surround sound, you can have a fantastic gaming experience with a console, in your living room, while sitting on your couch. Call me "old-fashioned," but I still prefer the comfort and seclusion of my office, my custom-built PC churning away as I game with mouse and keyboard, while I watch the action on a 22" dual-monitor setup, and listen to it all in 5.1 surround sound.

▪During the early stages of my evolution as a PC gamer, I established and religiously maintained my "$100" rule▪

Very simply put, I committed to the idea of never spending more than that amount on any *single* component or "mod," (modification) because I believed that this was the best way to keep my head out of the technological clouds, and prevent myself from spending too much money on mods to an existing system, when what I should have been doing was building a *new* system. I also focused on acquiring better *skills*, rather than better *components*.

For the most part, I consider this strategy to have been a great success, although in some cases it has led to the purchase of several components, when I could have simply bought the *right* one the first time. Had I done so, according to my second rule, which is "Buy bigger, buy smarter," I would have ultimately been both richer and better off.

Your particular budget may dictate a $10 rule, or a $20, $50, or even a $500 purchase limit. Whatever budgetary rule you establish by choice or circumstance, always remember that there is a very fine line between *optimizing* your system, and completely rebuilding it, and it is *very* easy to cross that line. It is also very expensive, as you will find that many of the "ultra-cool" mods and components you bought to optimize your old system will *not* "Frankenstein" over to a new build. Some will, but most won't—the technology simply won't be there. Ask me how I know. The benefit of my experience is what I am offering you with this guide, <u>but I cannot help you if you will not take my advice</u>. Therefore the take-away from this discussion is simply this:

▪Establish a modding budgetary rule or guideline, and stick to it▪

If you are a console gamer, there is not really much you can do to gain any particular "advantage" via hardware. There are some high-tech controllers you can buy—these offer customizable multi-key press programming options, and there are game-specific controllers you can acquire as well. If you have the budget, you may consider investing in such things, or putting it out there to those who love you that these would make great gifts for you at your next birthday, or other holiday occasion.

Of course you will want the latest and greatest console, with adequate memory, and good internet connection speed. As with the PC platform, if you are a smart shopper, you can find great deals on hardware by simply waiting until the next generation of a particular item is released, then snapping up the "old" technology at a bargain price.

Assuming that you have a decent console and an adequate controller now, you are pretty much good-to-go. You will still want to read the rest of this section, as you may become a convert to the PC perspective, and you will want to know what you are up against, on those games that allow console and PC gamers to compete against each other. With that said, the hardware section of this guide is primarily devoted to the PC gamer, or "real" gamer, as we like to call ourselves—no offense to console fans intended.

However, here is one simple concept to remember about hardware and settings configuration:

▪It is possible to optimize your setup for each individual game you play, and it is to your advantage to do so, no matter what hardware or platform you are running▪

Some games are "monsters," and will insatiably consume every bit of processor speed you have, and every hertz of your GPU, (<u>G</u>raphics <u>P</u>rocessing <u>U</u>nit) regardless of what you have "under the hood."

I still remember how excited the gaming community was at the release of *Doom 3*, and its subsequent expansion packs, because of the degree of visual complexity the game offered, versus anything else that had ever been released. This one game probably did more to push the limits of GPU design than anything had ever done before, as manufacturers rushed to produce hardware that was capable of displaying this intricate title properly, even on "medium settings."

At the time, most PC gamers had at *best* a single 256 meg (megabyte) GPU, and those were quite pricy. Within months, manufacturers were releasing 512 meg cards specifically designed for *Doom 3*—some even said so on the packaging. These "state of the art" cards cost as much as $500, and people still lined up to buy them! On the bright side, this made it a great time to get what *had* been a cutting-edge 256 meg card just last week, and that is exactly what I did.

On that note, there are some gamers who become "technology addicts," always chasing the latest and greatest hardware upgrade, looking for that smallest "edge" in competitive gaming. Much like an addiction to anything, there is no fulfilling that "need," because:

▪There is always going to be something bigger and better, and if you take this path, you will *never* be satisfied with what you have▪

A much better course of action is to learn to overcome whatever limitations your particular hardware may put upon you, and to wisely determine the additional benefit that a specific modification may provide.

For example, my first hardware upgrades were a budget video card, (128 meg!) additional memory, and a low-end sound card, along with some external speakers. These few (and inexpensive) mods *vastly* improved my gaming experience—my games went from "Meh," to "Wow!"

The beautiful thing about upgrading your system is that so long as you have not destroyed the hardware by abuse or neglect, you can always use the parts in another build, or donate them to a less fortunate friend, (or charity) as I have done with most of my hardware purchases over the years. My backup desktop PC, for example, is still running the quality 2.1 speaker system I bought 12 years ago.

Many games will very optimistically list a minimum hardware "requirement" on the box, and if you know anything at all about gaming, reading those "minimum specs" may literally make you laugh out loud, because if you actually tried to run the game with the specified hardware, most likely you would end up watching a *very* boring slideshow.

Since boredom is not what most gamers are after, you will want to optimize your system for gaming. If you have a decent PC setup now, even if it is only an "off-the-shelf" unit, you can do so without spending your rent money or college tuition.

For example, heat buildup is your enemy, and overheating has killed far more PC components than any virus ever did. Heat also causes your system to slow down, as many CPUs (Central Processing Units) will automatically "throttle down" to compensate for heat build-up. Gaming is one of the hardest jobs you can task your PC with, so step one in optimizing your setup should *always* be:

▪Keep your system cool▪

My first PC, the aforementioned *emachines* unit, was set up in the corner of my office, in my upstairs loft. I had placed the tower unit inside a desk cabinet, and would only open (and close) it to push the power button. One day, after a couple of hours of gaming, I felt very warm, and not just from the thrill of victory. I opened my cabinet, and I was hit by a blast of heat from the tower. It was so hot that I literally could have cooked food on top of it. Remember that this case was your basic steel box, the kind that most PC's were built with at the time.

This was a completely stock PC that I was running at 100% capacity, while keeping it inside an enclosed desk! I was lucky that I did not destroy my $900 system that day, although I am sure I shortened its life considerably—both the power supply and motherboard failed within months. **The take-away from this is simply that you *must* provide as much ventilation as possible for your system.** In this situation, I started trying a variety of scenarios to do so, first by drilling several holes in the back of the desk, behind the tower.

Later I took the cabinet door off to allow in more air, and ultimately ended up cutting the entire back off of the desk. None of these solutions worked perfectly, even after putting a box fan behind the desk. I finally took the tower out of the cabinet, and put it on top of the desk, with an external fan directed at it. This resulted in a case temperature that was merely warm to the touch, but left me listening to the tower and a fan grind away while I was trying to game, so it was not an ideal setup.

Does your current configuration resemble what I have just described? Is your tower hot to the touch, especially after you have been gaming for a while? If so, you need to start here. Even if you own a high-end, specially-built gaming PC, one that is designed with the cooling of its internal components in mind, you still *must* ensure that the *external* environment allows those components to do their job. You may even want or need to relocate your "game cave" to another, cooler location within your home.

Even if your case feels cool on the outside, your CPU may be running warm or even very hot when you put your system under stress. To easily determine whether this is so, boot your system up after you have not used it for a while, perhaps overnight. After *Windows* loads completely, wait about five minutes, then re-boot your system, only this time boot into your *bios* (<u>b</u>oard <u>i</u>ntegrated <u>o</u>perating <u>s</u>ystem) by pressing the "delete" key on your keyboard repeatedly until you see your boot screen.

Once there, look for a tab that says "PC Health" or something similar, then select that tab. Arrow down to "CPU temperature." Make a note of this number, and also of a nearby one called "Case temperature." These numbers should read in degrees centigrade, or "c." These are your baseline, or "cold" system operating temperatures.

Now task your system by doing something CPU-intensive, like gaming, or video rendering. Game for a half hour or so, or burn a home movie onto a DVD, while running a virus scan. When you have finished, re-boot into your *bios*, as above, then check (and note) the same two temperatures as before—CPU, and Case. Now you have a "stress," or "load" temperature to compare with your baseline.

If there is more than a 25 degree difference between them, or your CPU load temps show at, near, or beyond 70c, **then you need to address your cooling situation sooner rather than later.** Even if the difference is only 15c or so, you still may want to optimize your cooling, because cooler components will run faster, and last longer.

If you are not afraid to open your case and touch the things inside, and you have not already done so, one of the most cost-effective "mods" you can do to your system is to add cooling fans to the case, and perhaps even to change your CPU cooler to a more effective aftermarket unit. Be sure to "balance" the airflow going into the case with that coming out, for it will do you absolutely no good at all to have numerous case fans that are incorrectly positioned.

▪There are several good articles online that you can read on this particular subject, but to put it very simply you want to have sufficient air movement around and through your internal components▪

One easy setup is with four fans. Place one in front of the case, blowing air in, and one in back drawing air out. Put one on top to exhaust heat, and finally one on the bottom bringing cold air in.

Most modern PC cases will have room (and pre-drilled holes) to mount at least a couple of additional fans, perhaps even several, and the fans should be marked for direction of air flow. If they are not, plug them into a live connector, <u>then put an arrow indicating air flow direction on the fan with a marker</u>. This will come in handy later if you move your fans around, or to a different system.

Read the reviews and check the specifications for the fans that you are considering purchasing. Some are quieter and more efficient than others, as in the same size fan will move much more air than a competitor. It may also cost a few dollars more, but the investment is worth the cost, considering that these relatively cheap components will be protecting some very expensive ones.

Use the largest, most powerful, and *quietest* fan that will fit in each position, and that you can afford. In general, you will want to maintain a slightly "positive" air pressure level inside your case—that is, a little more airflow *in*, than out, because this will reduce the accumulation of dust inside your case.

Water or "liquid" cooling is another option, but I have no personal experience with it. For me, the "marginal" improvement in cooling ability that most liquid cooling setups offered was not worth the additional cost, complexity, or *risk* associated with locating *liquid* inside my case, in very close proximity to components that can cost hundreds of dollars each.

Even a liquid-cooled system is vulnerable to environmental conditions, so if you have not addressed those first, (as detailed in the previous section) you will not be gaining much if any advantage by going this route. For example, my current system sports two linked GPUs, a fiercely-overclocked CPU, four hard drives, four sticks of high-speed RAM, (<u>R</u>andom <u>A</u>ccess <u>M</u>emory) and more, and even after hours of gaming my system and board temps remain well within operating specs, and my case is barely warm to the touch.

All this is while cooling entirely with air. Of course, I do have a proper gaming case—these are instantly recognizable because they are typically large and well-ventilated, with mesh sides and top. I have a powerful aftermarket CPU cooler, and *seven* case fans, in addition to the internal fans that any good GPU will sport. These typically are designed to vent the heat from the GPU directly out of the case at the rear. Modern case designs locate the power supply at the bottom instead of on top, and they also vent the hot air that they produce directly out of the case, instead of releasing it inside.

Case fans can be purchased online from vendors like *newegg.com* for as little as $5 apiece, and a decent aftermarket CPU cooler can be found for around $25 on sale. This small investment in time and money will go a long way towards optimizing your hardware setup. Make sure to follow static electricity buildup prevention protocols when working inside your case, (always ground yourself by discharging any static electricity) and if needed you can use a cheap wrist strap to ensure that you do not damage any critical components.

Once you have installed additional case fans and/or a CPU cooler, re-test your system for baseline and load temps. They should show a substantial difference, 10c cooler or more. If they do not, check your fan configuration again, and make any necessary adjustments. In certain circumstances, a "negative airflow" (more air going *out* than in) configuration will be the better option, as in your temps will be lower. Just remember to clean the dust out of your case more often if you go this route.

▪If you will be replacing your CPU cooler, be sure to properly apply a good thermal compound, like *Arctic Silver*, or you will damage your processor▪

If your budget is at or nearly zero, you can still make sure that you have good airflow in your case by using cable ties to secure your power supply wiring properly, and by cleaning dust out of and off of your internal components. Adding even *one* small fan can help a great deal, so if that is all you can afford, find a cheap one with free shipping, and install it on the side of your case, facing towards your CPU, if possible.

▪Motherboards and Mods▪

If you will be working inside your case anyway, now is a good time to examine and make a list of the other hardware limitations that you may have, because step one in optimizing your hardware setup should *always* be to check your motherboard's expansion port (or "slots") capabilities *before* purchasing any external mod or component.

You can do this without even opening your case, by searching out your PC model online, and looking for the motherboard "details" or specifications list. Here you will see an explanation of what ports are on your board, and what is in them now. Alternatively, you can download and install a free program called *CPUID*. (See *Key Concepts* for a complete description of how to use this wonderful utility).

You will want to note your CPU socket size and type, memory (RAM) capacity, speed, and number of slots, and whether or not you have an "integrated" GPU. Take good notes at this point, and perhaps save a "systems specs" file on your desktop, because all of this information will be useful to you down the line, and it will help you avoid costly mistakes.

▪Nothing is more useless and frustrating than purchasing a component for your system, then discovering that you do not have the correct port for it▪

You can avoid this uncomfortable situation by doing a little homework before you start any mod project, and it never hurts to "refresh" your memory each time you do, by double-checking your specifications, and carefully planning for the future as well as the present.

Some components, like GPUs, will be available in all port formats, some (like sound cards) in one and not another. Therefore you will want the most critical component to go in the best available port, then work down the line until you have no expansion slots left.

Most motherboards will have at least one available "PCI" (Peripheral Component Interconnect) expansion port, and hopefully a "PCIe" (PCI "express) port or two as well. PCIe ports come in "speed" ratings of "X1," "X4," "X8" or "X16," and you should have one or more of each. If so, they may be different colors. They may also show a secondary designation of "1.0," "2.0," and so forth. The X16 will have the most "bandwidth," and the higher the secondary designation, the faster it will capable of transferring data.

PCIe X1 ports are instantly recognizable because they are very small. PCI ports are medium-sized, and typically are white in color. PCIe X4-X16 ports are the largest, will be the same size, and are sometimes color-coded. If you are uncertain about a particular slot, motherboards usually have labels by or near every port to identify them, but you may need a magnifying glass to read the tiny print.

Although an X16 3.0 GPU will run in an X8 1.0 port, it will not perform at anywhere near its rated specifications, <u>therefore typically you will want to match your GPU upgrade to the best available port on your motherboard</u>. Make sure that you do not install an X16 card in an X8 slot, unless you will be "linking" them. However, having more GPU capacity than your current board will support is not necessarily a bad thing, since it will be "forward compatible" to a better motherboard, should you acquire one in the future.

▪Replacing your motherboard should not be necessary unless it is defective, or you are building an entirely new system▪

You certainly do not want to replace a perfectly good motherboard just to accommodate a single new component.

If you also plan on upgrading or adding a hard drive, be aware that few if any boards still use the "IDE" standard for hard drive connectors, although some of the older models ones will have an IDE port available. Hard drives typically connect via "SATA" ports, and these also may show a secondary numerical designation—the higher, the better.

Most modern systems have decent motherboard sound capability, but will not have enough GPU guts to satisfy the average gamer, so upgrading your GPU, or "video card," should be the first easy (and giant) step towards optimizing your gaming experience. Again, please do not fall into the "hardware trap" of believing that all you need to succeed as a gamer is more and better "stuff," because that is certainly not true.

On the other hand, for example, if you want to host a baseball game, you must at least have a bat, a ball, and a glove, although these do not have to be the newest and best ones around to have a good time playing.

For the longest time, my rule of thumb in adding any single component was the "$100" rule I mentioned earlier. If what I wanted to add cost more than that, too bad. I waited, shopped a little harder, or lowered my standards a bit. Your particular budget may allow you to have a "$500" rule, and if so, more "power" to you, but it is possible to make a very nice gaming PC out of the one you have, one that is capable of running most all modern games at decent speeds and resolutions, without mortgaging the house or selling any of your children.

Wisely allocated, as little as $40 to $250 worth of components added at once or over time will exponentially improve your hardware capabilities, starting with cooling and a power supply, then adding GPU ability, perhaps memory, sound, a monitor or monitors, and finally a better CPU. The system that I have now cost about $2000, all in, (over three years) and I have not made any significant changes to it in over a year. It is entirely custom-built from the case out, but nothing in it is "state of the art" by any means. My system will run any game thrown at it at maximum settings across the board, with very few exceptions.

▪The key factor when deciding what hardware modifications to make or forego is always going to be "cost versus benefit," with the goal being to obtain the most bang for your buck, with each mod▪

Assuming you have your basic "bone-stock" system, off the shelf, with a decent CPU, the process you might follow would be this, in order, from least to most expensive:

▪Optimize cooling and airflow, add fans and an aftermarket CPU cooler.

▪Purchase a specialized gaming keyboard and mouse.

▪Install a bigger power supply.

▪Add an "off-board" sound card and upgraded speakers, plus a microphone, or headset.

▪Upgrade memory, always in pairs if possible, using the same brand and specs.

▪Upgrade GPU to the *best* PCIe X16 card the wife/SO and budget rule will allow.

▪Upgrade your monitor to a 22" (or bigger!), or add an additional monitor/s.

▪Overclock or upgrade your CPU.

▪Add an SSD (solid state drive) of at least 60 gigabyte capacity.

Depending on your individual priorities and budget, you may want to skip one or more of these steps, or perhaps re-order them. In my case, I have yet to add an SSD, and I upgraded my monitor at step 4, to a 22" specialized LCD model. The reason was that gaming on a 14" CRT monitor versus a 22" LCD is very simply a night and day difference, if only because on a tiny monitor you will *never* be able to run any of the advanced settings that your fancy hardware is capable of producing.

The monitor I chose offered 1680 by 1050 resolution, which equates to a 16:10 widescreen ratio, (also good for viewing movies in HD) a 20,000/1 dynamic contrast ratio, and a 2 millisecond (*ms*) response time. These numbers may or not mean anything to you, but the basic rule of thumb to remember when selecting a monitor is that you want *more* contrast ratio, and *less* response time, with the emphasis probably falling on response time. 5*ms* is the "slowest" speed you would probably want for a gaming monitor, unless we are talking about *Tetris*.

At the time, this single monitor cost over \$350, but you can now get a pair of similar (or bigger and better) monitors for that price. On the subject of multiple monitor setups, there are drawbacks to the "dual" setup, and one of them is that your center field of view puts your sight reticle on the bezels where the two monitors meet.

You could tweak the settings a bit to make the reticle slightly off center, and overcome this issue, but it might be better to wait and just go with a three-monitor setup, which I am told is amazing to see and use. However, dual 22" monitors look awesome, plus they give me a maximum viewable resolution of 3300 X 1050, and that is pretty sweet.

I only recently added the second monitor, mostly for work purposes, *cough* but coincidently my gaming proficiency and the overall experience were also greatly improved, a happy side-effect. If you already have your cooling, keyboard, mouse, and controllers where you want them, you may want to step up to a larger monitor, before anything else, as I did. A decent 22" can be found for less than \$150 now, delivered, again from *newegg.com,* or most major electronics retailers.

As with all components, <u>I suggest that you stick to name brands with good reputations, and always read the reviews before you buy</u>. Pay special attention to the available connectors each offers, as you will be bummed out to discover that you lack the particular adaptor or cord needed. You will also want to be aware of reliability versus price—as the very cheapest monitors can cost you more over time, because you will replace them more often. Mine came with a three year warranty, but I have had it almost five years now, and it still does not have even one dead pixel.

▪Keyboards, Mice, and Controllers▪

I will stay away from making specific brand recommendations as much as possible, because any well-known manufacturer will do. Specialized gaming mice and keyboards will add a lot to your gaming experience, and will improve your efficiency *if* you properly configure them.

With that said, what exactly is a "gaming" mouse, controller, or keyboard? And why would you want them?

Very simply, they are just PC interface devices that are optimized for gaming, either by virtue of pure speed, or configuration flexibility. USB joysticks, steering wheels, and even foot-pedal controllers are available, but these are typically designed and used for a *specific* game. It is usually not *necessary* to purchase them, although you may choose to do so.

Many gamers who like to fly combat vehicles or flight simulators, for example, will choose to use a joystick, as this closely approximates the actual flying experience, and adds realism to the game. Like all such components, pricing for specialized controllers can range from reasonable to unreachable, depending on your budget, and the features that you desire or expect. A good value in USB joysticks is the *Logitech Extreme 3D Pro*. I used this model for years during my *MechWarrior* days, and found it to be a fantastic accessory to have, mostly because it allows you to configure firing buttons for multiple weapons systems.

For years now, I have used a special "one-handed" keyboard for gaming—it is small and round, and is obviously not intended to type documents with. Although it is currently discontinued, it may still be found online, and you can find it using the search term: *"Wolf King Gaming Keyboard."* If you can find one, even used or "refurbished," I highly recommend the *Wolf King*.

One desirable feature found on some gaming keyboards is backlighting. A backlit keyboard is obviously much easier to work with in a room darkened for gaming, although technically you should not be looking at your keyboard while you game anyway, and if you are, most likely you are being "pwned." Other cool features of specialized gaming keyboards include some degree of ergonomic design or curvature, and perhaps even some macro programming ability, allowing you to combine multiple key presses into a single function. You should be able to get a nice gaming keyboard for as little as $40 to $50.

My mouse is a "wired" high-resolution laser unit, capable of "shift on the fly" changes in DPI (Dots Per Inch) resolution. In other words, it is extremely fast and accurate, and enables me to move my sight reticle from one side of the screen to the other with just a very tiny wrist movement. It also has extra buttons that can be customized for combat. DPI switching capability is important when it comes to changing gaming modes, for example, from a land vehicle like a tank, to a flying vehicle like a helicopter gunship.

In this case, I find that I like the fastest possible DPI speed for the tank, but a somewhat slower speed for the gunship, because (at least for me) extremely fast changes in direction while flying tend to end badly, and helicopters don't like to fly upside-down, in general.

If you asked 100 gamers what the "best" mouse, keyboard, or specialized controller was for a particular game, you would probably get 200 answers, because every gamer would give you at least two—the one they *have*, and the one they *want*. All such gaming peripherals come in "wired" and "wireless" versions, and there are those who swear by both. I use only wired components, because I have been on a never-ending quest to reduce "lag" issues to the absolute minimum, since I began noobing up the gaming universe.

It is said that wireless devices add just a tiny bit of "latency," or lag to your response time, and that is from the time you hear the twig snap behind you, until you turn to face "Shankey McShank" with his knife in hand.

▪Very expensive wireless devices may exhibit little or none of this latency, and you may simply prefer to use them▪

I have found that, dollar for dollar, and feature for feature, you get more for your money with wired peripherals, and you do not have to worry if it was the lack of "skill" or "lag" that got you shanked just now.

Some "pro" gaming keyboards costing hundreds of dollars will do just about everything for you except bring you a sandwich and your favorite beverage. They offer programmable "macro" features, (basically allowing multiple key press functions to be accessed by pushing only one key) backlighting, and some now even have touch screens in addition to the usual keypad. I've never owned or relied on anything this fancy, for two reasons:

Firstly because I never had the budget, and if I did have an extra $200 laying around, I bought a new GPU or other "important" component or two.

Secondly, I didn't think that relying overmuch on "technology" to overcome my lack of "skill" was much of a good idea.

Remember the lesson from the introduction? Put another way, you could say that:

▪When you have skill, good hardware will help you get better. If you don't have skill, no hardware can save you▪

With that said, certainly having better "tools" will make developing your skills *easier*. Most likely, any player on any game server that you would call "pro," or "leet," (elite) is not running around "pwning" the neighborhood on a bone-stock desktop with a 14" monitor. This player would at least be using a system with a larger monitor, and a decent "aftermarket" keyboard and mouse (or specialized controller). I would say that if you have those few things, and the time to practice, (along with a good attitude) you can become an "pwner of n00bs" as well, even if you *never* upgrade your hardware beyond this point.

One point to mention here is that it never hurts to ask such leet players this question:

"Exactly what mouse, keyboard, controller, or GPU are you using, kind sir or ma'am?"

Most pros are more than happy to tell you what masterful or meager devices aided them in your destruction, and some will actually wax poetic about their *"Pwnermaster 6000 GTI"* mouse, with interactive macro programming and real-time strategy analysis feedback capability. Of course, I made that last part up, but I *have* heard people describe hardware that I did not even know existed. Others will say, "Oh, I just use whatever was in the box when I bought my system."

I tend to disbelieve those who make such claims, if only because at a minimum you will want to upgrade to a proper gaming mouse, or other specialized controller, **even if that is the only mod you ever make to your system.**

Gaming mice and GPUs make perfect birthday or holiday gifts, as they are not too expensive, are small and lightweight, and do not cost much to ship. So if your budget is tiny or non-existent, you may want to put the word out about a particular item that would "positively thrill you" to have.

Shameless as it may seem, I have even sent out emails to people (who had asked me what I wanted, of course!) with hyperlinks to a particular product, and told them "Something like this would be awesome!" **If you do this, you might want to include links to three different mice, (or whatever component) for example, from low to high-priced**, so that your "giftor" can choose one that suits their budget, and whichever one you get, you will be happy with, because you picked out all three. Everybody wins!

How do you think I got my groovy keyboard? Yes, it was a gift—a much-used and appreciated one, at that.

▪Power Supplies▪

One of the most frequently overlooked modifications to your system (and perhaps *the* most important) is the power supply. Most stock PCs will arrive with a power supply that is at best "adequate" for the components that the machine contains, and even "adequate" may be a little optimistic for a system that will be operated at or near 100% capacity for hours on end. Even mid-range systems, with decent components, frequently contain very low-budget, no-name power supplies. Keep in mind that every single component inside your case draws power. Every stick of memory, every hard drive, every external card, *everything*.

The very first component that failed in my first PC was the power supply. It is fairly easy to diagnosis a power supply failure of course, because there is no boot-up, no beeping, no little flashing lights—no nothing. After a few months of gaming, (and the addition of two "off-board" components, plus additional memory!) the poor little thing just couldn't make it up the hill any more.

If you experience this type of failure, it is very easy to jump to the conclusion that something major or drastic has failed, like your motherboard or CPU, but it is usually just the power supply, **so check this component first, before you start tearing your whole system apart**.

My little power supply was a no-name 250 watt unit. When it failed, I decided that this was a good time to learn about power supplies, and of course to shop for a replacement, and it was now that I learned that if you add more "stuff" to your system, you need to add more power. Sort of a "derp derp" revelation, if you think about it, but keep in mind that this was my first PC, and I knew quite literally *nothing* about them.

•I learned that power supplies are an important part of a PC's breakfast, because they are the foundation on which everything else is built•

Like any foundation, you want a strong one, and you must design or allow for the biggest "load" that you will put on it—or plan to. Power supplies come in many shapes and sizes, or "ratings," ranging from the aforementioned 250 watt, to 1000 watts and beyond. You should choose your power supply based on the demands that you will put upon it now, or *plan to* in the future, and this led me to the second mistake that I made in my PC hardware "learning curve."

This mistake was in thinking that a PC power supply was like a light bulb, since they are both rated in "watts." That is, a 450 watt supply would constantly draw 450 watts, as would a 750 watt supply, and so on. Thus I saw no need to pay the energy cost associated with a 750 watt supply, when I only "needed" a 450 watt.

The "reality" of the power supply problem is that they supply what is "needed" at any given moment, up to their maximum rated capacity. If you are word processing or web browsing, for example, your supply is most likely taking a "coffee break," in that it is not "working" in any serious way. When you fire up the latest, greatest combat game ever, your supply must now "wake up" and work at or near 100%, just as many other components will have to, like your CPU and GPU.

The moral of this story is that you can usually find a good deal on a 750 watt or even larger power supply if you shop smart enough, even though your present system only "needs" a 500 watt supply. Ideally, you want to choose a supply that can *exceed* the future requirements that you may put upon it, as in the mods that you "plan" on implementing, versus just the ones you already have. An even *better* rule of thumb is to choose the biggest supply that you think you will need, (and can afford) and then go one size bigger. In the words of the ancient wise man:

"It is better to have, and not need, than to need, and not have."

If you follow this strategy, "Buy bigger, buy smarter," you will avoid the mistake that I made, which was in having to buy multiple power supplies, first a 450 watt, then a 500 watt, then a 750 watt, and now I find myself "needing" an even larger one. In other words, I could have just bought the "right" power supply a couple of years back, and only paid for one, instead of four.

The particular nuances of power supply selection are the same as with any other component, buying smart, reading reviews, understanding your present and future needs, plus a few additional considerations. Some supplies offer "modular" cabling ability, whereby you can connect and disconnect only the wiring that you need for the components that you have, thus reducing the clutter (and improving airflow) inside your case.

These are usually a bit pricier than the "non-modular" type, and they also offer the small risk of disconnection, (perhaps at a crucial moment in your gaming history?) if one of the cables vibrates or is jarred loose. Therefore I have always used the "non-modular" type, although your budget and needs may dictate otherwise.

Power supplies are also rated for "efficiency," and certain ones will show a number or "color" rating for efficiency, that is, the amount of power *in*, versus the amount of power *out*. More efficient units are "greener," and will cost you less money to run. You may see such labels as "80+ Bronze," "Silver," or even "Platinum Certified." These will cost you more money to *buy*, so keep that in mind.

They also may show a number of "rails" on which the rated power is delivered, with the "single-rail" being the preferred option for most system builders. Very basically this means that the supply is capable of delivering its entire rated output over one cable, an important factor if you will be powering one or more power-hungry GPUs, for example.

Be sure that any power supply you choose has enough connectors, of the *correct* type, to power any and everything you have now, as well as what you plan on adding to your system later. Most GPUs will require at least one "PCIe" connector per card, and some of the larger ones take two, *each*. Therefore you would need a supply with at least four such connectors, if you will be, or plan on "linking" multiple GPUs together.

Yes, you can "adapt" pretty much any connector to fit pretty much any component, but if you buy the correct supply in the first place you will not have to do so. Plus, having to run to the local "parts shack" during a system build is very annoying—ask me how I know.

▪Sound Cards▪

Adding an "off-board" sound card can do a lot to speed up your system, and improve your gaming experience. Most low to mid-range systems will have motherboards with *basic* sound rendering ability, but the factor to keep in mind about them is simply this:

▪The less work you put on your motherboard and CPU in terms of rendering video and sound, the more you free them up to do what you want them to do, that is, getting your game on▪

You have to be careful when adding sound cards and other peripheral devices inside your PC, because each device will have "drivers" that must also be installed in order to run correctly. Some manufacturers have a reputation of producing devices that have "issues" with their drivers, and these issues may cause conflict with other devices.

▪With that said, I have found this general rule to be the most effective▪

When installing a new component, do *not* install the software that comes with the device, unless you are specifically instructed to do so. If you have bought wisely, and you have done your homework and read the reviews, you will benefit from the experience of those who have gone before you. They may say such things as "Do not install the drivers that come with the device—get them from the manufacturer's website." This makes a great deal of sense in many cases, because typically the first thing you will want to do after installation is upgrade to the latest drivers anyway.

Creative is a very well-known maker of sound cards and devices, and I have had very good luck with their basic card, the *Sound Blaster Audigy*. It's cheap, (about $30) easy to install, and most systems, even basic ones, will have at least one PCI expansion slot. This card works very well, does what it is supposed to do, and does not cause issues if properly installed and configured. Again, if you have any system that is "mid-range" or above, or you have already upgraded your CPU, memory and so on, you may find little or no benefit in adding a sound card.

▪Basic, off-the-shelf systems will gain the most from this type of upgrade, and if that is what you have, this is a perfect mod to make▪

On my custom-built system, I attempted to go with a pricy aftermarket sound card, but I did not notice any significant difference in sound quality or system performance versus using my upgraded motherboard's onboard sound.

Therefore, a fancy sound card is one component you will not find inside my case, although I may still add one in the future.

On the subject of sound, most modern games are designed and optimized for 5.1 or better surround sound, and the gaming experience you will have is largely dependent upon the quality of the environmental sounds that you hear, or *don't* hear. Shankey and his deadly blade will never reach you if you hear that twig snap early enough, but if you are relying on a basic two-speaker desktop setup, or low budget set of headphones, you will *never* get the most out of any game.

▪Most modern games allow for "teamchat" capability as well, which means that you are capable of (and expected to) communicate with your squad or teammates via voice chat, and for this you will need a microphone in addition to whatever speakers you may have▪

There are some very nice gaming headsets that you may use, for both PC and console gamers—these offer very detailed, realistic surround sound, plus an integrated microphone. I have such a headset, but I prefer *not* to have the weight of one on my head for hours on end during marathon gaming sessions. I use a decent standalone microphone, along with a 5.1 surround sound system to get the best possible auditory experience.

You can find these components using the $100 rule, or even better, meaning that if you shop smart enough you can get both a decent 5.1 speaker system and a microphone, or a very nice headset, or even all three, for less than that amount. If your budget is very limited, you can find a low-end microphone for just a few dollars.

▪Video Cards, or GPUs▪

This is perhaps *the* most important component for any serious gamer's system. Beyond an adequate mouse, (and power supply) if you are only capable of adding a single "mod" to your system (because of budget or other restrictions) then this is the one you will want to make. Again, if you have a basic, off-the-shelf system, most likely you are now running your video applications (including games) with your "on board" GPU. These are usually "adequate" for older games, and even some newer games, if properly configured, as will be discussed in the *Settings* section. However, even adding a "budget" card, by today's standards, will vastly improve the visual and overall quality of your gaming experience.

I was literally amazed by the differences in resolution I was able to run once I added my first "aftermarket" card to my system. I saw things that I had never seen before. Details like rivets on machines, fog, and scowls on your enemies' faces will now become apparent to you. As with any component, there is a broad range of products available to you, from the very basic, to the "state of the art." If your budget puts you into the latter category, most likely you will not be reading this guide, but remember that, as always, hardware alone will *not* magically transform you into a "pwner of n00bs."

There are two chipset platforms on which most all GPUs are built, NVIDIA, and AMD. "Brand names" for each are varied, and many manufacturers offer cards based on both. With that said, most gamers are religiously devoted to one or the other, and in general, NVIDIA-based cards will cost you more than AMD. Both are engaged in a constant battle to "one-up" the other, if only for sheer bragging rights, as both chipsets now offer a great gaming experience, even with their low to mid-range offerings.

For the longest time, I used only NVIDIA cards, and I have had nothing but good luck with them. They are reliable, stable, and typically run cooler than AMD cards.

Some will say that their drivers are also more stable, and more compatible with other components. My very first off-board GPU was a 128 meg *GeForce* card, and I used that card for over five years, in various desktop PCs that I built, before I finally bequeathed it to a friend in need. It was running like a champ when I gave it away, and to my knowledge, it still is.

▪There are many manufacturers of GPUs, or "brand names," and as with any component, you will want to stick with well-known makers, and read the reviews before you buy▪

Different card makers also have different warranties, and restrictions on "modifications" that you may make, AKA "overclocking." The manufacturer may void your warranty if you overclock the card, so be careful if you buy a "cheaper" card with the intention of overclocking it to reach a higher performance level.

In *some* cases, this is a great strategy, but in others, you are just as well-served to wait for a better card to go on sale, or for a newer release to force the price point down. Add to this the option to "link" certain GPUs together for even more processing power, and it is easy to see how quickly you can add "monster" video processing ability to your system. (NVIDIA calls this process putting your cards in "SLI," and AMD calls it "Crossfiring").

Is this necessary? The answer is that it *may* be. As with the aforementioned *Doom 3* game, the latest and greatest games practically require you to have a powerhouse card or cards to run them at anything approaching their designed capabilities.

However, a little-known but important fact about GPUs is very simply this:

▪Even "mid-range" cards long ago reached the point of being "capable" of running most every game at "decent" resolutions and settings▪

Although manufacturers may *want* you to believe that you absolutely must have the latest and greatest card to be "competitive" as a gamer, <u>this is quite untrue</u>. As with many other technology-based products, like cell phones, once you reach a certain point, is there really that much difference between the version 3 and version 4? Your system and your budget are usually better off if you direct your mods towards other components that may be "bottlenecking" you at this point, like memory, or your CPU, for example.

Keep in mind that GPUs are the single most power-hungry component in your PC, and it makes *zero* sense to add a huge card to a system that cannot power it. You may also find more power and speed (for less money) by adding two smaller (identical) cards together in a "linked" setup, as I did. I am able to achieve decent frame rates, very high resolution, and an overall awesome visual experience using two mid-ranged cards, and I did so for less money than a single "monster" card would have cost me at the time.

On the subject of "frame rates," or <u>F</u>rames rendered <u>P</u>er <u>S</u>econd, (FPS) you will want a setup that is capable of delivering at least 30 FPS on a consistent basis, preferably much more, <u>for the game or games that you will actually be using the card for</u>. A very useful tool for determining frame rates and optimizing your system is called *FRAPS*. This wonderful free tool will be discussed in the *Key Concepts* section.

Keep in mind that it makes no sense at all to spend several hundred dollars on a GPU that will render anything you throw at it at 100 FPS, when the only competitive gaming you do is the occasional online chess match.

▪Likewise, it is unreasonable to expect a "budget" card to render the latest and greatest edition of the hottest game at 100 FPS▪

Between those two extremes, there is a "perfect balance" between what you would *like* to have, and what you *need* to have.

In general, I find that your GPU is one component that you should match to your *present* or near present gaming needs, rather than your distant hypothetical future need, and here is why:

Technology and competition both advance at such a profound rate that if you simply wait a few months, (or a year at most) the card that you "want" will become available to you, at a price you can afford. In general, cards advance quicker than games do, meaning that if you buy big and smart, you will get about three years of capability out of your card. Buying the latest, greatest GPU every year is simply wasted mod money, given that you could have allocated those dollars elsewhere in your system, and gotten much more bang per buck.

When comparing GPU specifications, there are several rating and performance factors to consider about each. Like many PC components, video cards are also marketed based on "bandwidth," and this is very basically the "amount" of information that a card can move through it in a given amount of time. An over-simplified analogy would be that of a pipeline between two buckets. Your monitor is one bucket, your CPU is the other, and the pipeline is the GPU. If your CPU holds five gallons, and your monitor holds five gallons, but your "pipeline" moves "water" at a rate of one gallon per minute, then it will obviously take five minutes to fill your monitor up.

In this case, "bandwidth" is the diameter of the pipeline, and it determines how fast the quantity of video data goes from point "A" to point "B." A larger pipeline may allow for the entire five gallons of data to move across in one minute, versus five, and so forth. In general, bandwidth, and memory capacity, (or how *much* "water" your card will hold) are the two critical factors to consider when selecting your GPU.

Cards are also rated using other criteria, starting with the "memory capacity," expressed in "megs," or megabytes. This will range from the abysmal 64 meg to the powerhouse 1000 meg and beyond. You will also see specifications for "bits" and for the "data rate" of the card's internal memory, and as with most things, more is better. A higher bit rate with a faster data rate is the preferred option in most cases, all other factors, (like price) being the same. For example, a "64 bit GDDR3" card versus a "128 bit GDDR5" card. If both were well-reviewed, from brand-name manufacturers, and cost the same, which one would you choose?

Two cards that are apparently identical, yet are for some reason priced differently, even from the same manufacturer, will usually display different specifications for bandwidth, and this is the factor that is less understood by the GPU-buying public. What you want to determine is: How much bandwidth do you actually "need?"

The answer has two parts.

The first part is that you need "enough" bandwidth. Enough to run the game or games that you have or want, at an *acceptable* frame rate.

The second part is: How much can you afford? As with most things in life, more is better, and more is also more expensive. Carefully balancing what you will *actually* be using the GPU for, versus what you can afford, will ensure that you get the best value for your mod dollars. With that said, here are a couple of examples of "mid-range" cards that will, (in a single card system) perform "adequately" for the majority of gamers, and both meet the "$100 rule."

AMD Sapphire Radeon HD 6670

Low Profile Bracket Included: Yes

Chipset Manufacturer: AMD

Core Clock: 800MHz

Stream Processors: 480 Stream Processing Units

Effective Memory Clock: 1000MHz (4.0Gbps)

Memory Size: 1GB

Memory Interface: 128-bit

DirectX: DirectX 11

OpenGL: OpenGL 4.1

HDMI: 1 x HDMI

NVIDIA ASUS ENGT440/DI/1GD5 GEFORCE

Chipset Manufacturer : NVIDIA

Core Clock : 822MHz

Shader Clock: 1644MHz

CUDA Cores: 96

Effective Memory Clock: 3200MHz

Memory Size:1GB

Memory Interface:128-bit

Memory Type: GDDR5

DirectX: DirectX 11

OpenGL: OpenGL 4.0

HDMI: 1 x HDMI

Both cards are priced about the same, and offer nearly identical performance specifications. When shopping for a GPU, you will also see references to "clock rate," "processing units," and "cores," and these will vary from card to card, chipset to chipset, and brand to brand. With these factors, more is typically better. In the examples above, you will notice that the NVIDIA card offers a slightly higher "core-clock" rate, and a much higher "effective" memory clock, (3200mhz versus 1000mhz), and that one references "CUDA Cores" versus "Stream Processing Units."

When you are considering two cards that are this closely matched in price and specifications, your choice will boil down to your preference for chipset, (AMD versus NVIDIA), power consumption, space available, and the output connectors available for each. In other words, you will want to look a little deeper than just the sheer "horsepower" offered by each. In these examples, one card is a "low profile" unit that is considerably *smaller* than the other. **If you have a "stock" PC case, most likely the larger card will not even fit, even if you have an expansion port for it.**

You also want to note the power consumption specified, whether multiple monitors are supported, **the maximum resolution they will display**, the warranty, and whether or not you can "link" the card to additional cards for increased performance. In this case, *neither* card can be linked, so if you "bought small" here, and were unhappy with the performance from it, you would not be able to enhance it, but would be stuck *replacing* it.

You will also want to *read the reviews*. Are the existing owners and users of the cards happy or unhappy? Did they have issues with drivers? Do they use it for the same types of games that you will? What frame rates do they report, and did they have any warranty issues? How were those handled?

▪A note here regarding reviews▪

Usually it is not necessary to read dozens of reviews for each item you are considering. Most likely that will be a waste of time. Read a few top reviews, and a few bottom reviews, but my experience has taught me that the most useful information there is to be found in reviews is in the "mid-range," or "three star" type. These are the folks who had *some* issues with the component, and were not entirely happy for some reason, but usually not enough to return and replace the item.

What issues did they have? Did the item not fit? Were the drivers "buggy?" Often you will find that extremely negative reviews come from folks who simply did not do their homework *before* they bought the component, and therefore they did not have the correct connector, or it did not fit, or they did not have the right port to install it, and so on. Most of these issues were entirely *their* fault, as all of that information can be found on the product description page, (if you look for it) and if not there, within the reviews for the product.

You *did* read the reviews before you purchased, right, Mr. Unhappy Consumer?

Often they have not, but as they say:

"Experience is a mother."

In summary, either of these cards will provide your basic bone-stock, low to mid-range system with a nice upgrade at a reasonable price. Something like this might be another item for your "wish list" around holiday time, if you do not have the budget for the item.

Keep in mind, though, that both of these cards are "dead-ends," meaning that they cannot be linked to enhance their performance, and therefore if you intended on performing such an upgrade later on, neither of these would suit you. There are, however, several cards in this price range that *can* be linked, and if it were me, I would seriously consider one of those, because this was my mod mistake number three, once I became a "serious" gamer.

▪That is, having to replace my undersized, under-powered, and under-capable GPU every year or so, instead of every three▪

If you use the "Buy bigger, buy smarter" rule when selecting your GPU mod, that is, a little bit *more* card than you "need," and you will not make this costly mistake. However, as mentioned earlier, if you know for a *fact* that your goal is to become an online chess grandmaster, and chess is the only game you ever intend to play, then obviously this rule would not apply.

▪System Memory▪

Most modern systems now ship with "adequate memory," although that term is very loosely defined when it comes to gaming applications. (Remember those "minimum specs" we laughed about earlier?). In the past, this was certainly not the case, as many stock PC's arrived with barely enough memory to boot up properly before lunch time, and some people *never* shut off their systems for this reason alone.

What is "adequate memory," as far as the PC gamer is concerned? Depending on your operating system, you may be limited to no more than three gigabytes of RAM (<u>R</u>andom <u>A</u>ccess <u>M</u>emory). This should be plenty for nearly all applications that you may subject your system to, so if this is what you have, look elsewhere for performance enhancements, then re-visit memory when you have addressed those other areas. If you are running an older system, it is very possible that you have one gigabyte of memory, or even less.

▪If true, this is a major bottleneck for your system, and one that you will want to resolve sooner rather than later▪

Fortunately, system memory has evolved so quickly that very good memory can be found at very affordable prices, and what cost $100 per gigabyte a few years ago is less than a third of that now. Memory should always be added in matched pairs, (or triplets, for triple-channel) if possible, as you will achieve the maximum performance boost this way.

You also must be very careful to match the RAM that you buy to your motherboard's ability to support it. Do an online search for your particular system's specifications, and within those specifications there will be an amount of memory listed that your system *has*, versus what it will *support*.

For example, your particular system's specs may show "2 gigabytes DDR2 800 RAM—4 gigabytes supported." Again, if your operating system only supports 3 gigs of RAM, (32 bit) then there is absolutely no point in adding or buying more than this, therefore the maximum useable upgrade to your system would be achieved by adding an additional gigabyte—still a substantial performance increase.

•On the subject of operating systems, most home-based PC's are running a *Windows* 32 bit version, although the trend is towards the more advanced 64 bit•

You can easily determine exactly what you have by going to "Start Menu>Control Panel>System." (Or by using *CPUID*). There you will see your current specifications. Look for your "system type," and if it shows "32 bit," then you are limited to 3 gigabytes of usable memory. How much do you have now? You will also find that information here. If you have anything *less* than two gigabytes, you will want to upgrade your memory before you do anything else, as far as optimizing your system for gaming is concerned.

Look for "Installed memory." If it says " 1 GB," for example, and you know that you have a 32 bit system, then you can quickly "turbocharge" your system by adding two additional gigabytes, *if* your motherboard will support it. It is here that you will find my PC hardware mistake number four, regarding memory "*slots*," versus memory "*size*." PC manufacturers have the annoying habit of building stock PC's with multiple sticks of smaller memory, rather than a single larger stick, because it is cheaper to build them this way.

Why does this matter to you? Because, for example, in the above scenario, where your system shows "1GB" of installed memory, most likely it will be in the form of two 512 meg sticks, not a single one gigabyte stick. If your motherboard "supports" 4 gigs, but only has two memory slots, (most now have four) then you will have to *remove* the two that your system came with in order to add any significant amount. Even if your system has four memory slots, most likely only two will be available to you without removing some of what is already there.

▪Therefore, in this example, assuming you have four slots, and two of them have 512 meg sticks already, in a 32 bit system the maximum memory upgrade you can perform will be obtained by adding two 1 gig sticks, for a total of three gigabytes of RAM▪

The take-away from this is that you will want to know what operating system you have, (32 bit or 64 bit) how much memory you have now, what type your board supports, (how much and how many sticks) and how many *empty* slots you have for expansion. You will want to know all of this *before* you buy any memory upgrades. If you do not know these things, you will find yourself in the position of making multiple (and costly) memory upgrades because you will be removing smaller sticks to free up a slot, thus subtracting what you removed from your total, and making an even larger upgrade necessary, or negating some of the value of that upgrade.

In my case, my first system shipped with (don't laugh!) 256 megs of total memory, composed of two sticks of 128 megs each, in a motherboard that sported two memory slots. Adding memory meant removing one of the existing sticks, therefore subtracting that amount, so my first "upgrade" of a single 256 meg stick only netted me 128 megs of *additional* memory.

These rules will apply no matter how many slots you have, and what is in them now. What I *should* have done was to add a single 512 stick, because my system "supported" a maximum 1 gig of RAM, so later when I discovered the "need" for still more RAM, I had to basically "donate" the now useless 256 meg stick that I had paid good money for only months before.

The lesson here again is "Buy bigger, buy smarter" when it comes to RAM, both because the prices are very low nowadays, and because you will be wanting (and needing) more of it anyway, so why buy RAM two or three times when you can buy the correct stick or sticks once? Memory is cheap enough now that basically you want to determine how much you have, how much your board will support, how much you "need," and then simply load your board up with as much as it will support and your operating system can use, end of story.

Again, if you have 3 gigs now, on a 32 bit system, there really is not much you can do in the form of a hardware upgrade to your memory, except perhaps by switching to "faster" RAM, but that is typically unnecessary, and if you are considering this route, you may as well start thinking in terms of a new operating system and motherboard (and therefore an entirely new system) at this point, as well.

Be sure to know and understand the "type" of memory your board supports, typically "DDR2" or "DDR3" and what "bus speed" (remember "bandwidth?") your board will support. While you are allowed to return or exchange RAM, it is a bummer to have to do so, when you could have checked all your specs carefully and bought the right RAM in the first place. Remember to always buy memory in pairs if your motherboard supports the "dual-channel" standard, and in triplets if you have the newer "triple-channel" type. Make sure to exactly match both the brand and specifications, and do not "mix and match" to save a few dollars.

Memory will also be rated in "speed" or "hertz," and again more is better, but only to the point that your motherboard will support. **Follow your system specifications closely, unless you plan on upgrading your motherboard in the future.** If you do, then be certain to "buy big" in terms of memory "speed," because your existing board can "down clock" memory to its maximum rated speed, but it cannot "up clock" to use any capacity beyond that.

As with all mod components, do your homework, shop smart, stick with major brands, and read reviews before you buy. Good name-brand memory can be found at very reasonable prices—about $30 for a two gigabyte upgrade kit.

▪The CPU▪

The "<u>C</u>entral <u>P</u>rocessing <u>U</u>nit" (CPU) is the heart as well as the "brain" of your system. It is the "Sun" around which all your other components will orbit. If you have a decent, modern system, your existing CPU will most likely be more than powerful enough to game with. If you have an older, "stock" PC, this may not be the case. Check your system specs (Start>Control Panel>System) again, and look for the processing speed and number of cores you have now. If your system has an older socket 775 Pentium in it, perhaps a single core at that, then you are definitely bottlenecking at this point, performance-wise.

The question is: Do you want and can you afford to do anything about it?

Before approaching a CPU upgrade, make sure that you have already overcome any other bottlenecks that may be holding you back, for the obvious reason that, much as a Ferrari and a Taurus move at the same speed in a traffic jam, your hot new chip will go nowhere fast if it must wait for other components to catch up.

Often adding other mods to your system, such as the aforementioned memory, sound, and GPU upgrades, will provide such a performance boost that an upgrade to your CPU will become unnecessary. It's very similar to a thoroughbred horse running with a 100 lb. jockey, versus that same horse running the same race with a 200 lb. rider.

Which rider do you think will turn in the faster time?

For this reason, performing a CPU upgrade was one of the very *last* mods that I did to my system, although I have upgraded it three times now, and that makes PC hardware mistake number five. All of these costly errors share the same DNA—that is, they are related to the "buy small" or "buy now" mindset, rather than the correct "Buy bigger, buy smarter" idea.

▪If you decide to upgrade your CPU, I would strongly suggest staying away from "used" components, such as you might find on "lists" or auction websites▪

These will not have any warranty, and could conceivably be infected with a rogue or malware program. This same concept would apply to RAM and GPU upgrades as well. The exception would be if you have a generous friend or family member who is upgrading *their* system, and they want to give you a "hand-up" by donating their "old" part, (but still better than the one you have), perfect.

You will need to determine exactly what CPU and specifications you have now, and whether or not any overclocking "headroom" exists on it. Some chips overclock surprisingly well, even the older "Celeron" types. See the *Key Concept* listing regarding a program called *CPUID*, for an explanation and a link to this very useful tool for determining what you have in your system now, and at what speed it is running. *CPUID* will provide you with much more information than would reading your systems specs from the control panel.

A very general rule of thumb would be that if your current configuration is anything less than a 2.8 ghz dual-core chip, you might want to consider upgrading it, *if* you have addressed your other bottlenecks, *and* your motherboard will support a reasonable upgrade. If your system *bios* and your current CPU both support overclocking, then you may want to squeeze out some extra performance here.

If you go the overclocking route for any component, use the online search term "overclocking (my chip) P4 Celeron 1.8," for example. Read the complete procedure and specifications that were used to achieve what level of overclock, and make sure that you completely understand any pitfalls that were encountered.

▪When overclocking, always use the experience of those who have gone before you▪

I keep referring to the poor sad P4 Celeron because that is what my first system had in it, and yes it did support some overclocking, but not on the stock motherboard that came with the PC. Since that board fried early on, (I can't imagine why) I had picked up a cheap aftermarket one to replace it. This board had some limited overclocking options available through the *bios*, so I used them. The 1.8 P4 Celeron actually shows quite a lot of "headroom" for overclocking, (I think mine was running at 2.8, or 3.0 ghz) but due to the other mechanical limitations of the chip, not a whole lot of performance increase was found.

Still, it was both fun and a good learning experience to "push" the little thing as hard as I could. Always ensure that you have addressed any cooling issues you may have *before* you overclock, because overclocking voids your warranty and stresses the chip with extra heat and voltage—not such a big deal with a $40 chip, but a *very* big deal with a $400 chip. You will want to search for your motherboard's specifications online, basically by using (for example) your *Acme Desktop 2005* as a search term. Once you locate your exact model, find the listing of the "details" or specifications unique to your system under "motherboard." You want to be aware of your motherboard's *exact* specifications to determine what CPU it is *capable* of supporting, versus what you have in it now.

You will see a listing for "socket type," as well as "Front Side Bus" (FSB) expressed in MHz, as in rated FSB "2000," or possibly 1666, 1333, 1066, or some other number. This is a good time to note the specifications for "supported memory" as well. Determine the exact speed and type of memory your board can handle, and how much of it. Upgrades to memory should *always* come before the CPU, *especially* if you currently have 2 gigs or less of installed memory.

The important factor is to *carefully* ensure that any CPU or "chip" that you are considering upgrading to is compatible with your motherboard, because if it isn't, you will now be in the uncomfortable position of needing a new motherboard to accommodate the new chip, (CPUs are *not* returnable, only "exchangeable") and if you will be replacing both your board and your chip, you are well on your way to building an entirely new system. <u>Avoid this costly mistake</u>.

▪Remember that building a new gaming rig is beyond the scope and intent of this guide▪

With that said, if you have determined that, for example, you have a motherboard that will support a "Socket 775 P4 Dual Core CPU, up to 2000 FSB," and you currently have an old P4 single-core Celeron, then obviously your system would benefit greatly by upgrading the CPU to a mid-range dual-core Pentium, and you would still meet the "$100 rule." Of course, you may also have a different socket type motherboard, either AMD or Intel, and if so, always consider these same important factors before performing a CPU mod, namely:

▪Have you addressed all the other bottlenecks that your system may have?▪

Would your system benefit *significantly* by upgrading the CPU, or would your mod money be better spent elsewhere, like on a new GPU, for example?

Remember that the GPU upgrade will take a substantial load *off* of your CPU, as in our "horse race and rider" example, so if you have not already performed this type of upgrade, you will want to do so *before* you look to your CPU.

Power supply, memory, and definitely a new mouse, plus keyboard and sound upgrades should all come before a new CPU, as should perhaps even a new monitor or two, in terms of enhancing your gaming experience versus mod dollars spent.

As with any component you are considering, always read the reviews carefully, make sure that the hardware you have now will support the part, and finally do a cost/benefit analysis to determine if that mod money would give you more benefit elsewhere. Then and *only* then should you consider upgrading your CPU.

▪The Solid State Drive, or SSD▪

First on my "to do" list for future mods, adding an SSD as a supplement to your system is said to provide a massive performance increase *in certain areas*. Boot times, for example, can go from 2 minutes to 20 seconds, and gaming software "load times" are also said to be greatly reduced. At this time, however, the technology behind the drives is still relatively new and untested, and failure rates are easily above 10% for some brands. Add to this the very high cost per gigabyte that you will pay, and the potential costs have thus far outweighed the benefits, at least for me. The drives themselves are known to be temperamental to configure, and can be problematic if installed incorrectly.

▪Therefore in my analysis the risk to my very stable, very fast system incurred by adding a tricky, unstable, and expensive SSD drive is too much to bear, at this time▪

Your budget of both time and money may allow you to add this component early on in the life of your system, and if you do so, it is highly recommended that you buy an SSD large enough to hold your operating system files, *plus* your gaming and the other files that you will work with the most. In addition, you will still need a "traditional" disc-based hard drive for data storage and backup. An SSD of at least 60 gigabytes, paired with a 1 terabyte platter-type hard drive, will provide you with the best of both worlds.

Some of the very newest SSDs are the so-called "hybrid" units, and contain both an SSD and a traditional hard drive. Some will even automatically "read" your system, and allocate programs and services to the correct part of the drive, according to "need." All this technology is very cool, of course, and also *very* expensive. If you have lots of money and time, this type of upgrade is something to seriously consider. If you have far more time than money, like most of us, you will want to address *all* of the other hardware issues and bottlenecks that you may have *before* you approach the SSD upgrade, because even an "affordable one" is still pricy.

In summary, this may be one mod that is best put off for when you *do* build a new monster gaming rig.

◄SETTINGS►

Now that you have your gaming *components* where you want them, you can begin to focus on your game *settings*. Much as it is easier to swim with both hands that it is to swim with one, it is easier to game with a correctly configured software setup, than with an incorrectly configured, or "default" one. What this means is that you typically will have the ability to customize your controls, video, and audio configurations for *each* game that you play, <u>and it is definitely to your advantage to do so.</u>

▪Control Mapping▪

Most every game will allow you to customize your movements, weapons selections, and other options through a process called "control," or "keyboard mapping." You may even be able to map the same function to several different keys or mouse buttons. You can follow two basic paths in doing so:

"Default," or "Custom."

The default movement, aiming, and firing keys for most games are very similar, and will follow a basic N, S, E, W pattern. The "W" key is typically set for moving forward, S for backwards, A for left, D for right. From there, your "shift" button might be used to jump, your CTRL button to crouch or run, and so on. Learning to game using the default keys is easier initially, but will harm you in the long run, because you will *never* be as efficient as you *can* be if you take the time to customize your keys and controls for each game.

Every gamer's perspective, style, and preference is different. You may have large hands, or small ones. You may be left or right-handed. You may like hand-to-hand, or "melee" combat, or you may choose to avoid it like a virus.

▪The point is that to have your keys mapped to your exact preferences, for each game that you play, will be and is the best strategy that you can follow▪

Customizing your keyboard and mouse configuration is the *best* method of giving yourself the proper tools for improving your gaming skills. During your evolution as a PC gamer, you will see the mapping of your keys change over time, as certain ones become more or less important to you.

For example, when I first started gaming, I found that med kits and health upgrades were something that I needed *very* quick and easy access to, so I would map those items to my Mouse 2 (M2) button—the "right click" option.

Doing so meant that it was very easy to heal myself, perhaps too easy, but it also meant that I was giving up the second-most useful mouse button for something that ideally one should not be using that often. Later on, as my skills developed, I mapped my "zoom" option to M2, and finally it has become my "melee" key, where it has stayed for years now.

Since I use a special keyboard, optimized for gaming, I do not use WSAD for movement, but have simply mapped them all down one place, because this made it easier for my thumb and little finger to reach other important keys. Therefore my basic movement keys are now SXZC, and I use this configuration for most if not all of the games I play.

Most games will allow you to map different keys for vehicles as well, and even separate keys for land versus air vehicles, but I typically use the same ones for movement on foot and in vehicles, across all games. The basic rule of thumb when mapping your keyboard, mouse, or specialized controller is simply this:

▪The more efficiently you map your controls, the more effectively you will use them▪

Therefore you might "rank" them in order of the most-to-least commonly used, and this will vary depending on the game, and whether you are on foot or in a vehicle. Mouse 1 (M1, or "left click") will *always* be your go-to key, and is usually best left as your "fire" button. M2 is your next easiest to use, so if it is health that you need most often, put it here.

As in my case, as your skills develop M2 may later become a scope zoom or melee button. If you have a specialized gaming mouse, (as you should by now) you will also have at least two or three additional buttons on your mouse that you can map.

On foot, I use those two buttons (M3 and M4, on the left side of the mouse) to switch between primary and secondary weapons, but in a vehicle, I use them entirely differently. One is to key my rear-view camera, (helps me spot those damn Snipers before they blow me up) the other my long-range zoom. This leaves M1 and M2 as primary weapons triggers, main gun, and machine gun, in my case. In a flying vehicle, you might want M3 as a "switch seats" selector, or even "drop bombs, with M4 as "release flares."

For those games that allow you to access multiple weapons, the "scroll wheel" is invaluable—just push and scroll to your weapon of choice. I also use "scroll up" as my scope zoom for most games, and "scroll down" as "reload." You will find that for most every game you play, the **reload** key will be very important, so map it *carefully*.

<u>Reloading your weapons continuously and without thinking is an important habit to develop</u>, because nothing sucks more than pointing your weapon at the enemy and hearing it go "Click!" After that, usually you will have about ten seconds to consider the value of keeping your weapon loaded at all times.

▪Keep an open mind and be flexible with your keyboard, mouse, and controller mapping options, and do not fall into the "default" trap▪

If you do, you will be allowing your games to train and calibrate *you* to operate *them,* rather than following the correct path, which is the exact opposite. Do not be afraid to stop, (mid-game if necessary) <u>and re-map a function to another, more useful location</u>. You may have to repeat this process several times, for each game that you play, but it will definitely be worth your while to do so, because you will notice an *immediate* improvement in your effectiveness.

▪Listen to what your eyes and mind are telling you your hands should do▪

You will find that some control configurations are useful across different games—for example, the buttons that you map for movement, "use," and aiming will most likely be the same no matter whether you are killing undead Zombies, or the deadly Shankey McShank.

▪Audio and Video Settings▪

Your video and audio settings, however, most likely will *not* be, simply because different games will put different demands on your system, in different areas. Keep this in mind:

▪One game may run perfectly well at "maximum" or "very high" settings, while the next struggles along like an over-burdened donkey at those same settings▪

Thus you will engage in a "trial and error" strategy for a while, as you determine the best and proper configuration for *each* game that you play. To easily determine this, look for an "options" or "settings" screen the moment your game loads up.

Some modern games now have a "Select optimal settings for your system?" option that you may be tempted to choose. Others may offer a "Scan your system's hardware capabilities?" option, or something similar. Among these, the most useful one you may find here is the "test" settings option, whereby a short action scene from the game will run, on the settings you have selected, and you will be shown a "results" screen, with FPS rates highlighted for various areas of the scenario.

Look for the "average," "high," and "low" FPS rates shown, as these are your most useful tools in configuring video resolution settings for each particular game. If the game does not offer the "test settings" option, (and even if it does) you may still want to use the *FRAPS* program from *Key Concepts*, (or something similar) to determine your system's optimal performance settings for each game. Start the program before you load the game, and watch the frame rate as you play. It should stay more or less consistent, and that is your goal:

▪Find the optimal frame rate for *each* game that offers *both* consistent performance and speed▪

Of course this is subject to the "minimum" performance standard that you find acceptable. For most gamers, this will be at least a consistent 30 FPS, and a good rule of thumb is that you should use that number as a *minimum* standard, not the "average" one. If you do so, you will be happy with your system's performance throughout your gaming experience. If it does not maintain this rate, you will want to perform additional "tweaks" to your settings so that it does, or look at upgrading a component.

▪Aspect Ratio and Resolution▪

Aspect ratio is very simply the proportion of height to width of your monitor or monitors, or of the image displayed on it or them. Each game may have a setting where you select either "4:3" or "Widescreen" for example, but typically you will want the widescreen setting, as most gaming monitors are of this type. Most modern games are designed to be displayed in widescreen, but if you have an older game or monitor, you may have to select the 4:3 setting to make it display properly.

Your monitor will have what is called a "native" resolution, that is, the designed display setting for optimal viewing. This will be different for the various sizes of monitors that are available. Obviously you want the highest or "best" available setting for your monitor or monitors. Your goal is to match (as closely as possible) the native resolution of your monitor to a setting within each game's options menu.

Typically there will be an exact match, so if for example your monitor's native resolution is 1650 X 1050, look for those same numbers in the options menu. If the exact match is not available, choose the next closest one. 1650 X 1050 is the same as a 16 X 10 "widescreen" format, but some games offer only "16 X 9." Most people would not notice the difference between the two while gaming.

The bigger the monitor, the higher the "possible" resolution setting, but it will do you no good at all to have a monitor that will display 1920 X 1080, when you have a GPU that will not, <u>therefore you will want to select the highest setting that your GPU will allow</u>, and that most closely matches your monitor's native resolution.

Add to this that higher resolutions are more taxing of your system and *all* of its hardware, not just the GPU, and you may find yourself choosing a slightly lower setting in the interest of maximizing your gaming experience.

▪Step one in this process will be comparing your monitor and GPU specs side-by-side▪

Are their maximum display resolutions the same? If so, perfect. This means that you may *potentially* run a particular game at that setting. From the options menu of the game, set the screen size at your monitor's maximum resolution, then run the "test settings" application, if the game has one. If the test run shows a *minimum* FPS of at least 30, then you are on track to move on to more adjustments. If it shows less than this, you will need to back the display option down one setting, making sure to maintain your desired display "ratio."

If you are intent on running a game at the maximum setting that your monitor will support, but your frame rate is sub-par at that setting, then you know that most likely your GPU is the bottleneck, even if it technically "supports" the resolution that you are trying to run. At this point you will have to determine if you will address the GPU bottleneck with an upgrade, or if you will need to tweak your systems settings to accommodate it. A crucial decision you will have to make at this point is:

▪What is more important to you, video *resolution*, or video *performance*?▪

The two are directly related, and most gamers will choose performance over quality to a certain point. If it means more to you, (and makes a better gaming experience *for* you) to see everything as *big* as possible, then you can start to optimize the rest of your settings based on that perspective. If you would rather see things *better*, that is, with better frame rates and less lag, or latency, then you will proceed from that perspective.

What kind of gamer are you? Again, most gamers are very competitive, and are willing to sacrifice a little video quality for an increase in performance. Remember those "minimum specifications" on the back of your game's box that we laughed about? Those truly are based on minimums, that is, with every available setting for video display (and audio!) at the lowest level. Therefore, while it may be "possible" to run the latest combat game at those settings, why on Earth would you want to?

Consider a game viewed at 800 X 600 resolution versus the same game at 1650 X 1050.

Obviously a sizeable percentage of the image data is not available at the lower resolution. However, in this same situation, a good "compromise" setting might be 1200 X 900—again, we are looking for the perfect *balance* between quality and performance, based on what *your* system is capable of rendering.

For several years, I ran most of my games at settings one or two steps below the maximum, but still at a very good level of quality and performance. Only when I was able to build a proper gaming rig did I begin to demand more than that from my system. A good rule of thumb, assuming that you have an entry to mid-level machine, and that you have optimized your hardware to the best of your technical and budgetary ability, is to start tweaking your game settings from the "middle" level. If your game offers a "default" setting of perhaps "medium," then that is the perfect place to start.

I still do not recommend using *any* default settings, because within each setting there are options that you might not want to give up, and there are some visual effects that will matter more to you than others. If you make minor adjustments in one or more of these areas, you will be able to increase them in others, perhaps even to the point of stepping up your overall display resolution by one level.

▪The goal of tweaking your software settings within each game is to ensure that you see and hear the maximum amount of information your system is capable of delivering to your eyes and ears▪

In other words, if you see and hear the enemy *before* they see or hear you, you are a lot less likely to get "pwned," and this whole process starts before you even set foot on the battleground. It starts on the "options" menu, and it is not finished simply because you have settings that will run at an acceptable rate. Once you begin playing a particular game, you will want to revisit the options menu a few times to "push" certain settings higher or lower, according to your experience within the game, and any subsequent mods you may make.

▪The settings "tweak cycle" process sounds complicated, but it really is quite simple▪

Remember that rendering high-quality sound and video is very taxing for your CPU, so if you have not yet added sound and video cards, for example, and your system is struggling to do what you want, therein lie two easily resolvable bottlenecks.

As you begin to tweak your settings, revisit the *Hardware* section of this guide, and ensure that you have addressed all of the areas your budget and skills will allow, starting with the easiest and cheapest, then moving forward. Every little bit helps—every pound you take off of your thoroughbred's back means that he can move that much faster.

Quick and easy bottlenecks to fix are memory and sound, and an investment of $50 or so here will go a long way. Have you already upgraded those components? Then look to your GPU for performance increases at this point, or perhaps a CPU overclock.

If you have a decent GPU, or you are unable to upgrade it at this point, then you will have to work with what you have, and here is where the other available video settings tweaks will become important.

Some are crucial, and some are just "eye-candy" that you get the feeling meant more to the game *designers* than they do to the game *players*. Does it really matter if I know that the paint is scratched on my tank? Or is it more important that I know how far away the edge of the cliff is?

▪With that said, here are some settings that may be available for you to tweak, in your quest for more eye candy and better performance▪

I will list each one, define it briefly, then talk about why it may or may not matter to you. <u>Some games will have only a few of these, and some may have them all, plus more</u>. Regardless of the *number* of possible settings adjustments, taking the time to tweak each available one of them for maximum performance will definitely deliver a better gaming experience for you.

Additional information regarding tweaks and settings for *specific* games is available online by simply searching "tweaks (your game) settings." For *very* advanced users, additional tweak settings may be accessible through the "console" of a particular game. These types of adjustments are made in the "input" side of the game code, rather than on the "output" side as the visual effect is rendered by your GPU. If you are interested in learning how to do them, use the search term "*console* tweaks (your game) settings."

You can use these console tweaks to squeeze out the very last fraction of performance from your GPU and system. Be careful if you go this route, as some changes within the game code will cause freezing, stuttering, or other performance issues with the game, and perhaps even with your system.

▪Vertical Synchronization▪

Sometimes called "V-Sync," this setting will fall into the "important" category, as it will make a significant difference in game performance, especially for lower-end systems. Vertical synchronization is basically a setting that imposes an upper limit on the rate that images are refreshed or rendered. Enabling this setting will tie your FPS to your monitor's "refresh" rate, so a monitor that refreshes at 60hz will only display 60 FPS, or less.

It is a way to "stabilize" the graphical images that you see, and level out the "ups and downs" that you otherwise might experience between an intense battle scene involving everyone on the server, for example, and a "mano-a-mano" knife fight with Shankey behind the barn.

In this example, your frame rate might drop to 15 FPS in the huge battle scene, but increase to 120 in the knife fight. Enabling V-Sync won't make much difference in the lower end, but it will "level out" the highs from the slower scenes, giving you a more consistent visual experience overall. This may or may not matter to you. Ideally, you should have your settings configured such that you never have to endure *any* scene at 15 FPS, and if so, you are less likely to notice the ups and downs, because your game will be running at a consistent render rate, anyway.

"Buffering" of this option is sometimes available, as in "double or triple buffered." Buffering allows two or three frames to accumulate before they are released to the monitor, again this function is designed to smooth out overall video performance. Enabling it may work against you if you are frequently moving quickly from slow scenes to extremely active ones, and vice-versa, as your system will struggle to put the image pieces back together for you.

▪Anti-Aliasing, or "AA"▪

This is another setting designed to improve the appearance of scenes by smoothing out the edges of a particular item. It adds an effect similar to "drop-shadowing" in photo-editing. A supply crate, for example, if viewed with AA off, will look very two dimensional and "square." That same crate, with AA on, (plus perhaps some other eye candy effects) may look very three-dimensional and realistic. AA, if available, will typically be selectable at a numerical setting from low to high, as in "2X" all the way up to perhaps "16X." The more of it you enable, the harder your system will work to produce and maintain it.

The key with setting the AA level is that if possible you want *some* of it, but not necessarily all of it. When you begin to tweak this setting, start at the minimum level. If your system is struggling to show you 30 FPS at this level, then you must turn the AA completely off. Not really a super big deal—you can live without it, as I did for years with my low-end system. Assuming that you can achieve a decent FPS rate with minimum AA of say 2X, then you can proceed to bump it up until you start to show significant drop-offs in FPS.

▪**This usually occurs quite noticeably from one setting to another, for example, your system may show you 45 FPS with 4X AA, but will drop to 20 FPS at 8X AA**▪

Obviously you will want to leave the AA at the 4X level, but remember, this setting will change from game to game, and while one game may die at 8X, another may run like a thoroughbred at 16X. <u>Avoid complacency with your AA setting, and always check your FPS rate when you get a new game</u>, with the goal being to "max out" *every* possible setting, *without* sacrificing performance.

▪MSAA, or "Multi-Sample Anti-Aliasing"▪

This is another variation on the AA theme, sometimes called "super sampling." It involves more digital analysis of a particular scene or item prior to rendering it, and therefore more workload for your CPU and GPU. As with AA, MSAA frame rates will tend to drop off quickly at higher levels, with some as the preferred option over none. Use the same method when tweaking this setting as you would any other—bump it up a little, re-run a test for FPS, then repeat. Again the goal is to have as much of it as you can achieve without sacrificing performance.

In general, you should start tweaking for MSAA one or two levels below what you would expect to get from AA, so for example if you know that your system will render most games at an acceptable level at 8X AA, then start the MSAA tweak cycle at 4X, and move up if you can.

▪Filtering Mode▪

This option refers to "Anisotropic" filtering, and is another setting designed to enhance the visual appearance of a particular item by rendering the pixel mapping in two or three different directions on the same object. Therefore it may be selectable as "bilinear" or "tri-linear." Bilinear is easier on your system than tri-linear, so if your frame rate is acceptable with bilinear, bump it up one setting. **If it is not, you may need to turn this mode completely off.**

▪Shader Detail▪

Changes to this setting may have more impact on performance than on detail. It is usually selectable between "Low" or "High," and will be especially noticeable in games that have scenes in or around water. Start your tweak cycle on the lowest setting, and move up from there if your system will support it. The differences between the settings are usually only visible to the most discerning eye, so if your focus is on "performance," rather than "quality," this may be another "eye candy" effect that you can live without.

▪Effect Detail▪

This setting represents a baseline for the depth and complexity that specific objects will be drawn to, and may have a significant impact on performance, depending on your system and the particular game. It refers to the number of "polygons" that are used in each object, and will be adjustable from low to high, as are many video settings. Start your tweak cycle on medium for this one, then go higher if possible.

▪Model Detail▪

Eye candy and polygons are the focus of this setting, as with effect detail, but there is usually only a very small performance hit in selecting the very highest setting, and very little difference in on-screen visuals. Start at "high," and adjust downward if needed, but there should be little difference in FPS between the various settings.

▪Audio Configuration▪

Various settings for audio effects are also typically selectable from the options screen of most games. As with your video settings, you will want to closely or exactly match your existing hardware to this option. You may see options for "environmental effects," or simply "sound quality," and these are usually selectable as "high," "medium," or "low." Keep in mind that while rendering audio *does* tax your CPU, the amount of taxation is not nearly as great as that created by rendering video. Think of it as more like a "sales tax," than an "income tax."

•What this means to you is that you will typically be able to select the highest possible settings for audio, regardless of the game you are playing, especially if you have added an off-board sound card•

Even if you have not, you will want to start your *audio* system tweaks from the highest settings, then move downwards from there if your frame rate is low, or you notice any stuttering, noise, drop-outs, or other unwanted audio artifacts. Sound effects volume sliders, as well as game music volume sliders may be visible on the audio options screen. These have no effect on performance, but they do effect your gaming experience, so configure them carefully.

Again, every game is different, and what is a "perfect" or "comfortable" setting for you in one game may be unbearable in the next. I typically keep "sound effects" at maximum volume, (because I *do* want to hear every twig snap) but music volume I set to 50% or less. Remember that these are "in-game" settings, and you will of course also want to adjust your system's output volume level as well, to your speakers or headphones.

You will also typically have the option to select the *type* of output for the audio, as in "headphones," "stereo" "5.1 Surround," or ("Home Theater") and so forth. Some games will auto-select the option for you, and will keep that selection in memory, so be careful if, for example, you have plugged in a pair of headphones for one game, then later decide that you want to hear the game through your 5.1 external speakers. They will still make "noise," but it will not be surround sound, and if you check your game settings you may note that they are still set to "headphones."

▪The take-away from this is to always "pop-in" to your settings menu and verify that your audio output source corresponds to what you actually want to hear, for each particular game that you play▪

I have gamed for days, perhaps weeks, with an incorrect setting, then was amazed by the difference in sound quality when I switched back to the "correct" output source.

◀STRATEGIES AND TACTICS▶

Now that you have your system hardware and control settings properly configured, <u>it is time to get your game on</u>. If you want to game well and not be owned, these first two basic concepts are *critical,* regardless of what game you play, your playing "style," and what player or character selection you make within the game.

Therefore you should study them *carefully,* and if you only learn two things from this entire chapter, make them the following: *Situational Awareness,* and *Tunnel Vision.*

▪Situational Awareness (S—H—K)▪

"Stay frosty out there!"

No doubt you have heard this phrase many times in war movies or simulations. The crusty, hardened sergeant (with the heart of gold) gives the new recruits this advice on their first day in battle, and pretty much every day after that. And for good reason—it's good advice.

But what does it *mean?*

Staying "frosty" and *situational awareness* both mean the same thing—being aware of *everything* that is going on around you, *all* the time. It is a heightened, almost "Zen-like" state of mind, where you are both *in* the game, (or battle) and *of* it at the same time.

For example, when you are moving from place to place, don't just fix your vision on your objective—look *around* you.

▪Getting to point "B" isn't really the objective—getting there *alive* is▪

Look *above* you. Look *behind* you. Listen to *every* sound you hear. Learn which ones are the "natural" sounds made by you and your team. Learn which ones are "unnatural" sounds made only by the enemy forces and their vehicles. Foreign languages are a "dead" giveaway here.

How many rounds do you have left? *Watch* your ammo indicator, or count your rounds as you use them. Running into a building and getting owned because your weapon goes "click-click" when you need it to go "Boom!" really sucks, especially when you subsequently get killed by the guy who had his *back* to you, but his weapon loaded—unlike you.

How much health do you and your squad have left? *Watch* your health indicator, and theirs too. You should be healing yourself and them *before* you engage the enemy again—it will be too late during the battle.

Why would you want to do this? Because if you think about it, in a perfect combat simulation, as in real combat, you would only have *one* life, and if you lose it, that's it. There would be no "re-spawning," or "resuscitating" you.

You're *dead*.

▪Therefore to avoid death, "real" soldiers (and pro gamers) develop a very finely-tuned sense of *situational awareness*▪

They see the smallest details in the environment around them. They know where their squad mates are, at all times. They know what weapons each is carrying, what damage they can do with them, and how much ammo there is to go around. They are aware of the direction of the wind, and the sun, because those things can also mean life or death.

It is nearly impossible to "surprise" them, because no matter which direction you approach from, someone is watching. No matter how quiet you are, someone is listening. In online gaming, these are the dreaded "pro" or leet squads that are always accused of "hacking," because they are *so* good.

Fortunately for you and I, combat simulation games are just that.

Games.

If you "die," no worries—you will "live" again. However, each time you die and re-spawn, you move your team a little farther away from victory, and the other team a little closer to it.

In some "round-based" games, like *Mechwarrior* and *Left for Dead*, you and your squad start out armed with whatever you bring to face the enemy squad. If one member is destroyed, that leaves one less to face the entire enemy team, sort of like a hockey team losing players to penalties—it's easier to score against a team with fewer players. In these types of games, there is no "re-spawning" until the end of the round.

▪Every game will offer visual and auditory "clues" about what is going on around you, and that is why you want your system configured well enough, and optimized, so that you can see and hear every possible cue you are given▪

I spend a lot of time in tanks, for example, and enemy soldiers have the annoying habit of creeping up to my tank, placing explosive charges on it, then gleefully blowing me and my tank into tiny wet pieces.

But if I am *listening*, I will hear the smallest "click" sound as the magnetic charge is stuck on the tank, and there may be two or three of these to ensure that enough explosive is placed to actually destroy the tank, not just damage it. Then there will be a tiny "beep" sound, as the charges are armed in preparation for detonation. All of these clicks and beeps are *not* the normal sounds my tank makes, and if I hear them, <u>because I am listening for them</u>, I will be able to dismount the tank and kill the enemy, preferably *before* my tank is destroyed, and even if the tank goes up, I can get another one.

If I go up with the tank—well, that's the end of me.

Things like a "missile lock" warning, or a nearby squad member's life indicator suddenly decreasing or disappearing are visual and auditory cues that your own death is probably imminent. If you hear someone shout "Grenade out!" in English, from behind you, and you are playing as a *Russian*, what do you think that means?

▪In certain games, much ado is made about using "comms" or "*teamspeak*" capability to cry for help when you are under attack, and you may be criticized if you do not▪

Certain squads and teams will instantly kick or even ban you if you do not have a microphone, or do not reply to the brusque "You got a mic?" question immediately. From my perspective, however (and from one I feel more closely approximates "real" combat) crying out might not only cause my own death, but the deaths of my squad mates as well.

Better still to *always* be watching your squad and teammates, <u>particularly their life indicators</u>. Many times I am already killing the creature or soldier that is attacking them as they are crying out for help. Why? Because I heard or saw the enemy approaching, and I was watching my buddy's back, as I *should* be doing, and as I *would* be doing, in *real* combat. Ideally they should be doing the same for me.

I would then laugh as they thanked me, and tell them, "Don't worry—I got your back."

▪Teams and squads filled with players who have a highly developed sense of *situational awareness* may go through an entire round without saying a word to each other▪

They blow through every enemy, every obstacle, like a well-oiled and finely-tuned combat machine. Conversation is unnecessary, because everyone understands the objective, and their own part in achieving it. Other times, the only "chat" you will hear is about the local sports team, (or bar) or a particularly funny joke.

These are the teams and squads that I prefer to join. They are more realistic to me. They may not be to you, but I do not doubt that you will enjoy the experience of being on one.

However, voice chat is *extremely* useful and necessary for "calling out," or "spotting" enemy players and vehicles, (in addition to "painting" them on radar) such as a brief "Tank at 2 o'clock!" or "Sniper on hill right!" When used for this purpose, voice chat can be crucial to maintaining your squad or team's *situational awareness*—keeping them alive, and winning battles.

Another legitimate use of voice chat or "comms" is to strategize and formulate battle plans, but even this is typically redundant or unnecessary, because many if not most games follow the same basic pattern:

"Go from point A to point B. Do so as quickly as possible, with the least loss of lives and resources."

The end.

Or, the goal might be:

"From point A, move to point B, capture it from the enemy, and do not allow the enemy to re-capture it. Proceed to point C, repeat."

The end.

Very simple objectives, if you think about it, really, but I cannot count the number of times I have been asked by a squad mate, "What's the plan?" or "What's the strategy?"

I will always reply with a sure-fire, four-word ultimate battle plan for victory:

"Kill more. Die less."

▪If you follow this simple plan, and everyone on your team does as well, you will almost always be victorious▪

Every war is ultimately a "war of attrition," with the objective of "wearing out" your enemy's economy and resources. They destroy one of your tanks, you destroy *two* of theirs. They kill your platoon, you kill their *company*.

"Indians," "Guerilla fighters," and even our own famous "Minutemen" all followed this very basic and effective strategy against superior numbers and overwhelming odds.

But to be successful at it, you must *see* the enemy before he sees you.

You must *hear* the enemy before he hears you.

You must *kill* the enemy–before he kills you.

If you have seen the movie *The Book of Eli*, the main character actually *smelled* the enemies who were trying to ambush him—before *he* killed *them*.

S.H.K.

See—Hear—Kill.

And *that* is what I mean by *situational awareness*.

▪Tunnel Vision▪

Tunnel vision is the **exact** opposite of *situational awareness*.

▪It is the absolute fixation on a specific player or objective, to the exclusion of all else▪

It is the one behavior you will almost never see a pro player exhibit, because they know it is what gets you killed and loses battles. Often a by-product of an "pwning," or of rage, a player (or squad) typically becomes tightly focused on the enemy player, tank, or plane that is repeatedly destroying them. Their game stats and kill ratio decline rapidly, as their confidence level hits rock-bottom.

Thus fixated, they do not see or hear anything else, making them even easier to kill and "pwn," and ensuring that this vicious cycle continues. If you find yourself with a kill/death (K/D) ratio of 0/10, (*zero* kills to 10 deaths) for example, then you definitely have developed a bad case of *tunnel vision.*

•If so, you need to immediately re-focus yourself by switching modes or even games•

If you are playing as infantry, for example, get into a tank. If in a tank, get out of it, and so on. This will force you to develop a new combat perspective, ideally one based more on *situational awareness* than on *tunnel vision.* Switching player *types* can be very helpful as well. If you are gaming as a Sniper, try a support role for a while. Focusing on helping your team succeed, (and doing well at it) will help you lose your *tunnel vision,* and rebuild your confidence.

•Another very unhealthy side-effect of *tunnel vision* is that to be owned repeatedly *will* destroy your confidence•

If you have no confidence, you will have no strategy, and this ugly, vicious cycle will continue. Thus you must take *immediate* action to end it, and if you see a member of your squad or team showing a serious case of *tunnel vision*— help them deal with it. Encourage them to focus on the entire team, rather than on a specific enemy, vehicle, or objective. *Tunnel vision* can infect anyone and *everyone* on your team, from the commanding General, to the freshest noob. **No matter who has it, it is never a good thing, so deal with and overcome it as quickly as possible.**

•Single Player Mode•

Most games will offer both multi-player and single-player modes through the menu. While you may be itching to jump into a multi-player server from the first minute you own the game, often a far better (and vastly underused) strategy is to learn the basics of the game by spending a few hours in single-player mode.

You will be able to familiarize yourself with the weapons, player types, and maps you will be using when you do go multi-player. You will have a "stress-free" opportunity to properly map your control options for weapons use and movement on foot and in vehicles. You can stop and re-map keys as often as you wish, and if you are getting owned by the AI, who cares? There is no shame in that. No one will ever know, and no "stats" are tracked for single-player mode.

▪All the weapons types and vehicles are typically available to you in single-player mode, allowing you to "try them out" before you are able to "buy" them by leveling up▪

Thus you will gain valuable technical experience and knowledge. Most every pro gamer I know spends at least a few hours in single player mode for *every* new game they acquire, if it is available. Why? Because they know that this is the *quickest* way to flatten out the "learning curve" of a new game, and the *best* way to minimize the amount of "owning" they are subjected to.

An often overlooked benefit to spending some time in single-player mode, but an *extremely* useful one, is the opportunity to familiarize yourself with the AI of the game, and the behavior of the Bots within it. This is *very* valuable knowledge that you will definitely want to take with you and use when you go multi-player.

Therefore, the take-away from this discussion is that you should *always* spend at least a few hours in single-player mode, preferably five or more, for every new game you wish to master.

▪Player Types and Tactics▪

Player or "character" types usually fall into one of four categories for most combat simulations:

▪Medics, Engineers, Snipers, (or "Recon") and Assault▪

Each will have different abilities and weapons that are available to them, and these will show up as part of your "Kit." You will have the option to select what items are available to you each round or "re-spawn," and more and better items will become available as you advance in rank and experience in a particular game. This process is called *leveling up*," and it is certainly to your advantage to do so as quickly as possible, at least to the point of gaining the items or weapons you want for a particular player type.

▪A "balanced" team will have good combinations of each type▪

An "unbalanced" team will be heavily-loaded with one particular player type, usually Snipers. Not only is this a bad strategy, but it has become so pervasive that some servers will even "limit" the number of a particular player type. If the team already has that amount, then you will not be able to choose that player option until a spot opens up. "Good" teams and squads (and "good" is usually synonymous with "victorious") will show an even balance of player types. "Bad" (and "bad is usually synonymous with "defeated") teams will not.

▪Use *situational awareness* to determine what player types are already on the team you are joining, and which one you should choose to best help your team achieve victory▪

Medics usually can heal or "revive" injured or dead teammates, so presumably it is a good idea to have at least a couple of them on a team, or at least one in your squad. Since "Medic" is *properly* more of a "support" role than an active one, often there will be few or no players willing to take the part—except those who are mainly concerned with keeping *themselves* healthy.

Medics can also periodically place health upgrades for other players. This is obviously better for your team, so if you choose a player type that can place health or weapons caches for your team, <u>do so early and often</u>. Do not wait for your team to cry for medical attention, or ammo, because if you do, it will probably be too late for them. Usually each player's status indicator will show the "need" for health or ammo, and this makes it easy to "do the right thing." Some noob players (and "pros"!) act as if health and ammo kits "cost" them something to drop, and will only do so when *they* need them.

▪If you see this happening, it is a good idea to remind your team and squad mates that health and ammo kits are *free*, and to supply them frequently▪

You will also get points every time someone uses the kit that you have dropped, and this will assist you with "*leveling up*," because the more points you get, the more items and ranks you will gain. I have finished rounds in the top five spots (or better) by simply doing nothing more than make sure that the "pros" on my (winning) team stay alive and well, and that their weapons stay hot, because they *never* run out of health or ammo. Supplying your squad with ammo or health upgrades usually rewards you with *double* points—another good reason to join a squad.

Assault player types will have some different weapons options available than Medics, usually a little heavier, perhaps even machine guns. They will also typically have the ability to supply their team with ammo, and as you would imagine, not having bullets, rockets, or grenades can quickly become a game-changer and battle-loser. Assault is probably the most popular player selection, if only because choosing this type means that *you* will never run out of ammo.

Engineers will carry the heaviest weapons, like mines and rocket launchers, and are your "go to" guys if there is a particularly pesky tank or flying vehicle that needs to be gone. They will also usually have the ability to repair your damaged tank or chopper, and will get points for doing so. As with other player types, Engineers are often "selfish" with their skills, and will run right past your critically-damaged tank or vehicle without even waving at you.

▪Apparently, your failure to plan on taking damage does not constitute an emergency on their part▪

Again, if you are an Engineer, and your teammates are crying out for "Repairs!" or "Protection!" from a particularly menacing vehicle, most likely it is too late for them—you have failed them, and yourself. So if you take on the role of an Engineer, be prepared for criticism if you do not actually provide defense and perform repairs—that is, do your *job*, and do not expect Medics or Assault players to consider your failure to plan for injuries and ammo shortages as constituting an emergency on *their* part.

Snipers or "Recon" soldiers are the final player type in most combat simulations, and are often the most common on the battlefield, for some reason. This type of player is obviously more of the "Lone-Wolf" kind than the "Go Team!" guy. Snipers cannot heal you, fix your vehicle, or provide you with ammo, and in my experience, the one thing they *can* do well is the thing they most often fail at—that is, spotting enemies at long range, and providing cover for tanks and weapons emplacements.

Because of the nature of the role, they frequently display chronic *tunnel vision*, and become fixated on their next target, to the detriment of their team. Many times I have been destroyed in my tank, not by a chopper or an enemy tank, but by (ironically enough) an enemy Sniper who has crept up on me and placed explosives on my tank. This while two or more Snipers on my own team are strategically located on hillsides <u>behind and above me</u>. You would think that it would be easy for them to periodically "watch my back" by looking to see if anyone is creeping on me, and at least "spot" them for me, if not kill them, but usually they do not.

They are far too busy looking downrange, trying to take out *one* soldier, and improve *their* K/D ratio, while the enemy is destroying one of their teammates *and* a tank, or an AA gun, or some other valuable *team* asset. This while they do not hesitate to cry for "Ammo!" or "Medic!" when they need either of those players to help *them*. For these reasons, Snipers are often disliked by their own teammates, as well as by the enemy. Therefore, if you take on the role of Sniper, keep in mind that you are still part of a team, with a *team* objective ("Victory!") and team responsibilities.

▪**If you do not fulfill them, do not be surprised if your teammates do not rush to assist you in your time of need**▪

You may also wish to locate yourself with or very near a Medic and an Assault player, so that it is easy for them to heal and resupply you, when necessary. Sniper school 101 teaches you to take a shot or two, then *move* to another position, yet too often a Sniper will find a particular hidey-hole on a map, and then camp there for the whole round. When they do, I am pleased to report their position to my own Snipers, and also to occasionally send them *back* to hell with a nice heavy tank round to the noggin.

▪Phasic Movement▪

"Phasic" very simply means "in motion."

In Bruce Lee's book, *The Tao of Jeet Kune Do*, he refers to a basic hand-to-hand combat stance he called the "*SPBKS*," which stands for S̲mall P̲hasic B̲ent-K̲nee S̲tance, with the emphasis on "phasic," as in, *always* in motion. He believed that keeping his muscles in a state of flux also kept them in a higher state of readiness, and that they would therefore move more quickly in the desired direction once instructed to do so, since they were *already* in motion. If you watch him on video, you will see his *phasic* combat philosophy at work.

Whenever he is facing an enemy, his entire body is in constant motion, from his feet to his head. He stands on the balls of his feet, not the soles, and "bounces" up and down as he shifts them back and forth. The movements continue at the knees and hips, and his torso rotates, while his shoulders and hands move back and forth. His head bobs and rotates, and even his *eyes* move from point to point, as he "sizes up" the enemy, and plans his next attack.

▪In combat simulations, as in "real" combat, remember that moving in straight lines often equals death▪

If you run in a straight line, it is easy to "lead" you, and you will quickly be shot down. The same principle applies to vehicles—those that roll, fly, or sit in one steady direction or spot are easy to focus firepower on. In tank warfare, I have learned that "parking" my tank in a particular place for more than a few seconds will quickly attract mortar strikes and tank rounds.

Therefore I keep my tank in constant motion—back and forth, side to side. Moving towards the enemy, firing the main gun, then backing up makes it exponentially harder for them to *accurately* return fire, as they cannot simply use the trajectory of your incoming round to gauge their outbound shot—it will be off by several feet or more. Even better is to fire the main gun *while* in motion, so the trajectory of the round relative to the position of my tank is different from the moment it leaves the barrel.

The best tankers in combat simulations, and presumably in "real combat," are those that can acquire and *accurately* target the enemy while moving at top speed. The days of using a tank as a glorified mobile artillery platform, as seen in old war movies, are long gone.

Likewise, when you are flying a combat vehicle, if you hover or circle in one place, you will be re-spawning in a matter of seconds. Watch pro pilots at work as they own your team. They move up and down, side to side. They move in small circles up, then down, then backwards. Hitting them is like trying to grab a greased weasel with your feet, and that is why their K/D ratio is so annoyingly high.

▪When on foot, *never* stand still▪

Always be in motion. Duck, jump, crouch, go prone. Move quickly from one spot to another in a zigzag motion. Remember that you *want* the enemy to shoot *at* you, because that will help you (and your squad) determine their position, and make it easier to spot and kill them. What you don't want is for them to *hit* you when they shoot at you. Don't be an easy target.

▪Be the smallest, quickest, and most difficult target that you can▪

Move from cover to cover, and remember that if you are one of many targets, you may not be shot at all. If you are the *only* target in a field of view, and you have been "*spotted*," then your lifespan may become very abbreviated, very quickly. This is one more of the many good reasons to join a squad—and stick with them. Squad mates are sometimes humorously referred to as "meat armor."

▪Squad and Team Strategies▪

Combat simulations are all very similar, and will fall into certain categories. They will typically involve either attacking an objective, or defending it. They may entail moving troops and resources out from point "A," which is often called your "main" or "uncap" base, meaning that it cannot be captured by the enemy. Many games will start out with a certain number of "lives" or "tickets" for each team, and some additional objective waypoints (B, C, and D) that may be captured and held. Squad-based games typically involve simply moving from point A to point B in the shortest possible time, with the least loss of life.

▪Possessing waypoints will cause the enemy's ticket count to deplete faster, or yours to deplete slower▪

Capturing (and holding!) all of the objective waypoints will result in a much faster victory for your team. This type of game is often referred to as a "conquest" or "capture the flag" round. You may have the option or desire to use vehicles like tanks or planes, or even fixed gun emplacements. You will also typically have the option to select the type of player that you will bring to the round, and this may vary depending on whether you are attacking or defending.

Other games may involve simply moving your team or squad from point "A" to point "B" as quickly and efficiently as possible. The team with the higher score for the previous round will go first in the next one. You objectives would therefore be to either reach point B with all the members of your team intact, or to prevent the other team from doing so. The quicker you stop the other team, the fewer points they will get for the round.

▪Assets like health and weapons upgrades are usually discoverable along the way from A to B, but the more time you spend looking for them, the more time the enemy has to re-spawn and destroy you▪

In this situation, you will need to balance your *personal* desire for more and better in-game "toys" with achieving the *team* goal of finishing the round intact, and beating the other team. I have seen members of a squad spend ("waste") 120 *team* (30 points X 4) health points to acquire a *single* health upgrade worth 30 points, not such a good use of team resources. However, if you are the opposing squad, using your "ghost" time during re-spawns to look for goodies is a great idea—just remember where you found them when it is your turn to run for point B.

In these types of games, if you get yourself or a teammate "killed" during the round, they will usually stay "dead" for the rest of the round. This leaves your team with a serious disadvantage versus the other team, which is why pro squads typically will target the noob (or the weakest player) on the other team for an "owning." It is the basic "domino" attack strategy. Push one over, then the rest will fall quickly. Knock the easiest one down first, then the rest will be that much simpler to take out. <u>This is why noobs so often feel that they are specifically targeted—because they *are*.</u>

A very basic and *effective* combat strategy, in "real life" and in all combat simulation games, is and always has been:

▪Attack the weakest target with your strongest weapon▪

On your typical squad-based, A to B type game, the weakest target is the newest player, and the strongest weapon is the most experienced player on the other team. However, since this is a known quantity, a "fact of life" if you will, this can be used to your advantage. If you *know* that the enemy will target a specific member of your team, or a specific asset (a tank, plane, or weapon) you can plan your defense strategy accordingly.

If you are the newest (least experienced) member of your squad, you want to avoid this common noob mistake at all cost, <u>and that is the tendency to lag behind the other members</u>. It is analogous to a cub or baby animal in the wild, following the pack or its parent. This is the smallest, weakest, and slowest target, and that is why they are so often isolated as prey.

▪If *you* are that noob, always ensure that you are at or near the very *front* of your group▪

You will not take point, because you do not know what you are doing, or where you are going. You do not want to be the caboose, because you will get owned, and will subsequently cause the death (by attrition) of your entire team. If you stay in the second or third position, or just behind the point player, you can watch and learn from them, and also earn some brownie points by covering their back, <u>as the point player is the second most popular target, after the noob</u>.

Keep this important lesson in mind:

▪Take care of your point, and they will take care of you▪

If you are the noob, first of all you have no business being on point, (remember "noob rushing?") and you certainly will not gain any experience or friends by causing the destruction of your team. If you are *not* the noob, and you know that your team has one, (or more) you should take it upon yourself to "babysit" them, as you already *know* they will be targeted for extra attention—I just told you.

Use this knowledge to your advantage, plan for it, and watch the noob's back *without* appearing to do so. This strategy will make it appear that you already know what the enemy is thinking, and it will negate the value of their attacks. It will also keep your noob alive much longer, and help your team achieve victory.

▪Resist the urge to quickly abandon the weakest member of your team▪

If you are going to do this anyway, you might as well immediately kick them from the team, and hope for a better player to join your squad, because leaving them behind means a death sentence. <u>Simply tell the noob to keep their focus on the point player, and to always stay a few steps behind them</u>. If they will take direction via comms or team chat, make sure they know the squad's strategy, and their part in it.

Likewise, counter-attacks are very effective when using the noob, or another player as "bait." One strategy that I have used effectively is to "trash talk" the other team, between (or during) rounds. Criticize their playing style, or player name, (in a friendly fashion, of course) their skill level, or what have you. I don't mean call people names, or cruelly belittle them, just entice them to target you, and to develop a bad case of *tunnel vision* focused on you. If they do, they will become much less effective as a member of their team, and you will have a definite advantage.

Simply tell your team, (privately) what you are up to, and that you are setting yourself up as a target. This will take attention off of your noob, and your point man, and is most effective if you are *neither* of those things. The other team will change their focus from the two easiest targets to you, and if you maintain a moving position that is very difficult to attack, like in the middle of your squad or formation, you will be essentially "untouchable," and the enemy will waste time and resources trying to do the impossible.

▪**Properly enacted, this *one* strategy has caused the destruction, demoralization, and subsequent defeat of more teams than any other, so learn it, and learn how to recognize when it is being used against *you*▪**

This strategy will lose effectiveness after a round or two, but if it does, simply change the focus of the plan by having a different member of the squad take the role of "bad cop," or "antagonizer."

▪Spotting the Enemy▪

Most games will allow you to "spot" the enemy when they cross your field of view, whether on foot or in a vehicle. Some will automatically "paint" the enemy with a red icon, visible to both you and your team for a few seconds. However, usually you will need to *proactively* spot the enemy by hitting a certain key that will then paint them on radar for your entire team to see.

<u>This is an incredibly important aspect to most combat simulations, and is one that is commonly overlooked by both pros and noobs alike</u>. Pros seem to feel that they do not "need" any help to spot the enemy, because of their highly developed sense of *situational awareness*. Noobs may not know *how* to do so, or how important it is.

In a contest between two evenly-balanced teams, matched down to the newest player, the winner will almost always be the team that does a better job of spotting the enemy. If everybody knows where that Sniper is, everybody can shoot at them. If every chopper knows where that tank is, every pilot can "drop the bomb" on them. The quicker you dispatch enemy vehicles and assets, the better off your team will be.

▪Remember that the "pro players" on the other team are their *most* valuable assets, so if you make their life difficult by constantly focusing heavy firepower on them, they will become much less effective against *your* team as they spend most of their time running for cover or looking for a Medic▪

Keep in mind that you will also get points for spotting the enemy, and more points if they are destroyed *because* you spotted them, especially by your squad. It is easy to amass hundreds of points every round by doing nothing more than spot enemies for your team, especially if you have a powerful scope or advanced optics, as I do in my tank.

The quick and easy strategy for developing a good sense and ability to quickly spot enemies is to properly map the key so that it is very easy for you to do so. Map the *spot* key to one of your mouse buttons, or to one of your "primo" locations on your keyboard, and *practice* hitting and using the key often. Some games will not only paint the target on radar when you spot them, but will also loudly announce the find in team chat—hearing "Tank spotted!" causes everyone to automatically look at their radar screen, and sure enough, there is that pesky tank they have been looking for.

One extremely useful technique I have developed is to learn to always hit my *spot* key repeatedly whenever I am sweeping a field of view, especially when using long-range optics or a rifle scope. Frequently the *game* will "see" the enemy sniper in the tree line 2000 yards away, even if my *eyes* don't. Radar will paint them, the game announces them, and very soon my squad will hunt down and kill the target—another step closer to victory.

You will be a much more valuable asset to your team if you learn how to *spot* enemies for them. You will level up faster, and your *situational awareness* will exponentially increase as you see enemies before they see you.

Remember:

See—Hear—Kill.

▪Cornering Up▪

"Put your back to the wall!"

This is another basic combat tactic, with its roots in the very first *Doom* game. You just ran into a room or combat zone filled with possible hostile forces? Find a wall, or a solid object, like a tank, or a rock, and put your back against it. This way you can be certain that any and all attacks and threats will come from one direction only—the front. Even better than one wall would be *two* walls, and thus the concept of "cornering up."

▪You and your squad will situate yourselves in a corner during heavy attacks▪

Thus situated, you can watch both the front, and each other's backs. However, in this position, you and your squad are vulnerable to "splash damage," or "massed attacks," such as many enemies at once, or a grenade tossed amongst you, for example. If this happens, the corner will serve to focus the attack or damage on you—if your *situational awareness* is telling you that this is happening (or is about to) then you will want to get *out* of the corner ASAP.

If the opposing team tends to corner up for defense, anticipate this on your next attack, and coordinate with your squad to deliver a massed attack or splash damage weapon into that cozy corner, turning it from a defensible haven against you—to a cold coffin for them.

▪Team Selection▪

As soon as you join a server, you will be able to check the score and stats for each team or squad, usually with the "Tab" key. If there is a great deal of variance between them, <u>most likely the teams are "stacked" with mostly experienced players on one team</u>, and mostly noobs on the other. Frequently the only opening will be on the noob team, unsurprisingly because of rage quits. If there is an opening on the "good" team, you will be able to switch to that team, and if you are a weak or new player, this will be your best strategy to avoid a confidence-destroying "pwning" by the stronger team.

▪Others will have this same idea, of course, therefore you may not be able to join the stronger team because it will unbalance the server▪

In this case you will have to choose either to stay and get spanked, or to leave that particular server and search for another, more evenly-balanced one. There are pluses and minuses to both strategies. If you stay, you will no doubt be "defeated" by the other team, but if you stay, you will be able to learn (by observation and osmosis) what successful strategies and tactics the winning team is using.

A mixture of both is probably best. For example, sometimes I will stay to try to help and strengthen a weak team, sometimes I will leave to be part of a "victorious" one. If your confidence level is high, stay and learn. If it is low, move on to another, stronger team that will be able to "carry" you a little.

▪Server Rules▪

Most every server will have "rules" posted that will be visible in a banner at the moment you join. The obvious ones like "no spawn raping," "no griefing," "and "stay out of uncap," are to be expected on most every server. Additional rules like "no camping," "limited player types," or "no team killing," may also be listed, and the punishment for violations is typically a kick or ban, either temporary or permanent.

▪If you are not willing to follow the rules of a particular server, either because you don't believe that "rules" are "realistic" in combat, or whatever, then it is better for you and everyone else if you simply move on to another, more accommodating server▪

For those gamers who have a tough time with rules, some servers even list "No Rules!" "No Whining!" Before you complain about an abuse you believe that you are suffering at the hands of another player, be sure to check that you are not on a "no rules" server, or one that does not prohibit the behavior you are seeing.

If the idea of "no rules" is attractive to you, stay and enjoy. If not, you may want to quickly move on, because "no rules" servers tend to be very "Wild West" in nature, will not have admins, and will often have very lopsided teams. Still, it is refreshing once in a while to drop in on one, if only to see how the "other half" lives.

▪Mod Servers▪

"Modded" servers are those that are running game code that was not initially part of the designed programming. These types of servers usually will very clearly state what mods are running and how to access them. Sometimes they don't, so be aware of them, especially if you see player types behaving in an unfamiliar way—moving too fast, or jumping too high, for example. Modded servers can be great fun, or they can be an awful "pwnfest" if not all the players understand the mods, and how to use them.

Be careful not to accuse players on a mod server of "hacking," because you will be laughed at, and rightly so. There is a big difference between a "hack," or exploit that is only available to a specific user, and "mods" that are available to all players, *if* they know how to use them.

▪Until you understand the *basic* mechanics of a particular game, you should probably avoid modded servers▪

Once you are familiar with a game, (and perhaps bored by it) you may choose to seek out mod servers, because they offer a new and exciting perspective on the game.

One very common mod is called *XPM*. All character types will have enhanced abilities and access to advanced weaponry, and will be able to "level up" using a points-based system. Points are awarded for specific actions involving attack or defense. You can then use the points to "buy" items within the round, such as weapons, or extra health upgrades, or even an extra "life."

Again, as with any server, if you join a modded one, look for an even balance of skill levels and pings. If you see that the other team has four "level 30" players, while yours has four level 10's—expect to be dominated throughout the round. On a positive note, you will get to see and experience a lot of cool character talents as they are being used to own you.

▪Effectively using the available mods will entail a process called "binding," whereby you map a specific talent or weapon "buy" to a specific key for instant access▪

While this is not necessary to use the mod, (commands can usually be issued through the "chat" menu) stopping to type "!Buy fheal" while critically injured during a mass attack is probably *not* the best strategy. Regardless of "level," the difference between the "pwners" and "pwnees" on a modded server will likely be found in the *effective* use of binds.

▪Latency, or Lag▪

On the server browser window, you will also see the "ping," or "latency" (lag) of each available server. The closer the server is to your physical location—the better your ping, and the less lag you will experience. Lag is measured in milliseconds, (*ms*) and a very good (and very close) server will ping at 50 to 100*ms*—perhaps even lower.

Once on the server, your own ping will be visible, as will the pings of others. Players with extremely laggy pings may cause the entire server to slow down, so always consider the pings of the <u>server, the other players, and yourself</u> when choosing which server to jump on.

▪As a general rule, an evenly balanced server will have all three numbers approximately the same—and ideally this number would be 50-100*ms*▪

Keep in mind that a 100*ms* ping is 1/10 of a second, or about an eye blink, so you will want to consider that when you are aiming at your targets. A 250*ms* ping is one quarter of a second, and that is an *eternity* in game time. You will "lead" your targets according to the ping they show, but this lead may either be ahead or behind them, as the server attempts to build "hit boxes" for both of you. You may have difficulty hitting someone with a ping that bad, and vice-versa. Complaints and accusations of "hacking," or "lag armor" may fly, in both directions.

Better still to avoid servers and players with extremely high pings, and in fact many servers will "auto-kick" players who exceed a certain threshold—usually 300*ms*. A decent time may still be had by all on a server with more latency, perhaps 100-200*ms,* but avoid servers with pings higher than that. The server lag, plus the inevitable player lag, will definitely make your gaming experience less enjoyable. This will especially apply if you are trying *not* to be the "pwned n00b"—who has not learned to compensate for lag.

▪Hacking▪

Let me preface this section by saying that I have *never* used any hack, glitch, mod, or exploit in any game, ever. My successes and failures as a gamer are entirely due to my skill, or lack thereof. I have absolutely zero respect for any gamer who does use them.

▪Latency and lag, and the way a particular game constructs "hit boxes" are easy to confuse with hacking▪

If your ping is 100*ms,* and you lead your shot based on that, but the player you are aiming at pings at 250*ms,* then you will in fact "miss" your target, even though *your* screen may show *you* a direct hit and kill.

With that said, accusations of hacking are frequent, and are almost *always* baseless. Great skill and an extremely highly-developed sense of *situational awareness* are often confused with hacking. Why were you shot dead with an instant one shot kill, the moment you rounded the corner? Because the other player *heard* you, or *saw* you, before you saw or heard them. They knew you would be there—and they were waiting for you when you got there.

That's why you are dead. Not because of hacking, but because of experience and skill. Ironically, one of the greatest compliments you will ever receive as a gamer is to be called a "hacker," because of the amount of "pwning" you are doing. Immature gamers are quick to throw such accusations around like so much over-ripe fruit at a bad play, but they are usually confusing (and excusing) their own lack of skill for "hacks" and "exploits" by the opposing team, or a specific player.

So if you get called one, (and you are not) just laugh and say "Thanks!" for the great compliment that it is to be named what you are not, because of your skill at "pwning n00bs."

▪With that said, there are unfortunately more than a few actual hackers out there, mucking up the gaming universe with their foul presence and bad behavior▪

Therefore you should learn how to recognize and report them whenever you see one. Again, be careful with your accusations, because "hacker" is a *very* offensive term to be labeled with—it's like being called a liar and a cheat at the same time.

Back in the "bad old days" of online gaming, a common exploit was called the "firewall" or "lag" hack. Game servers send information between your system and the other players. The speed of the transmission is affected by the pings of all the parties and the server. The data is sent in "packets," and if there is too much latency, the packet will "drop," and so will your awesome 800 yard kill shot. Latency can be *induced* by mapping a "stop all traffic" key for your firewall to your keyboard or controller.

Players who knew they had entered a "crapstorm" or other lethal situation would simply hit the key, and leave it on for a moment or two—enough time for the game server to drop the damage packet that you and your system would otherwise have delivered. Players using this tactic are usually easy to spot, as they appear to "teleport" or "skate" from one point to another, perhaps dozens of feet from where you last saw them. If you tab to the stats screen when you suspect this is happening, you will see their ping go from perhaps $100ms$ to $500ms$ or more, then drop back down.

The focus of this type of hack is to avoid taking damage *from* you, but most hacks are designed to deliver damage *to* the opposing player with an unfair advantage of speed, firepower, or accuracy. These are called "speed hacks," "wall or wireframe hacks," or "aimbots," and yes they do exist. Simply search online for the term "speed (or aim) hack (your game) PC," and you will find numerous videos and even websites offering to sell you the various types of exploits.

Speed hackers will move in an unnatural manner, and are also usually easy to spot, because they get too greedy with the hack. It can be "dialed-up" to whatever percentage the hacker wants, but anything over a certain amount is instantly recognizable for exactly what it is. A 100% speed hack, for example, would have the player moving at double speed, but a less obvious 5% to 10% hack may never be noticed, except by the sharpest eyes. It is still an advantage, but again, most hackers will want 50% or more, making them easy to spot—and to kick, ban, and report.

Wall hackers and "glitchers" will exploit the game code to place themselves "inside" a wall or object, making them immune to damage from others, then will "pop out" briefly to take a shot at the enemy, then back in the wall they go. Related to the wall hack is the "wire-frame" which allows players and objects to be viewed *through* walls, because it removes the game code that draws the solid wall, leaving only a "stick" or "frame" drawing, thus the name. You may think that you are cleverly concealed, but the hacker can see your silhouette through three walls, and yes, they will be waiting for you when you round the corner.

Aimbotters are also relatively easy to spot if you know what to look for. They tend to move and aim just slightly faster than everyone else. They will also commonly display ridiculous and impossible Kill/Death ratios, like 25/1 or even 50/1. Again, this is because of their lack of character and greed, because if they ran the hack intermittently, that is, occasionally turning it *off*, it would be much harder to detect them. If you really want to catch an aimbotter, join their team or squad, and tag along with them. You will then be able to "ghost" them while you are re-spawning.

•You will see them do such things as turn 180 degrees, aim, and one-shot kill an enemy, all in a fraction of a second•

If you watch closely enough, you can see that their sight reticle does not move in a "sweeping" fashion as it should, but rather from "point-to-point." Also, most gamers develop a high degree of proficiency with a particular weapon type, like an assault rifle. They will have one or two other weapons that they are good with, and the rest they will be OK with, or will not have used at all. On games that allow you to check a player's stats for weapon use, Aimbotters are easy to detect, because they will show the same *ridiculous* degree of accuracy with *all* weapons, like a 10/1 K/D ratio with the pistol, the shotgun, the rifle, *and* the rocket launcher. If the game has a water pistol, they would be 10/1 with that, too. This is because they are too stupid to turn the hack off when using uncommon weapons, and will use it for everything.

Fortunately for the 99.9% of the gaming community that wants to honestly own or be owned, most servers run "hacker detection programs" of one kind or another that look for suspicious behavior and known exploits, and will not even allow a player with modified game coding to remain on the server. Look for servers that offer this protection, and be wary of those that do not. The host may purposefully not use hacker detection, to allow themselves and others to use hacks against unwary players.

Sometimes these programs are "hyper-sensitive," and you may find yourself getting kicked for something like "Your game version does not match the current version," or something similar. If you are kicked for this reason, (and you are not hacking) you can usually fix this by updating your game manually, or doing an online search for "Kicked (your game) version mismatch."

▪Server or Squad Size and Composition▪

Servers are configured in accordance with the host's preferences, and the strength of their hardware and internet connection. Typically the most players you will see on any given multi-player server is 32—or 16 per side. The smallest number is usually 8 players, or 4 per side. The particular game itself may limit that number as well.

In general, if you are a weaker player with less experience, you will want to join servers with bigger teams, and more squads, because this will allow your skill level to "average out" over a larger number of players.

One "noob" out of 16 players is not a deal-breaker or game-loser, but one out of a four player team is a different animal. If the other team is 100% pro, and yours is 75% pro/25% noob, which one do you think is most likely to win?

▪On a larger team, joining a squad is a terrific way to gain experience, and to quickly "level up" in rank and status▪

If you join a squad, take note of the player types that are already on it, and be prepared to take on a "support" role in that squad, perhaps as a Medic or Engineer. Then do your very best to follow the squad leader's direction, and to re-supply, heal, and repair all of the assets and squad mates that you can. If you do so, you will learn quickly, make friends, and even win a few rounds or two.

Certain "Lone Wolf" types will prefer to form a squad, and then "lock" it, thus prohibiting anyone else from joining. This can work for and against you. If you like to operate a vehicle, for example, it will prevent players from spawning into your gunner's seat just as you are about to use that particular gun or position. Being seen as "not a team player" can work against you in that others may not feel that helping your one-member squad is much of a priority. More experienced players are often found in one-member squads, so if you are looking for a mentor, you may ask to join that squad, and offer to heal or repair for the squad leader.

▪Bots or "AI" Players▪

Some multiplayer games will populate a team or server with "AI" characters, or "Bots." These will be controlled by the programming within the game, subject to the code that has been written for them. To allow the game to continue when a human player drops out, a Bot will be inserted into the position left by the departing human player. You can tell which players are "real" and which are not by simply using the "Tab" key to check player stats. Bots will *not* have a ping.

▪There are pluses and minuses to having and using Bots on your squad or team▪

Many players will not start a round with one, but prefer to wait for another human player (or players) to join. When this happens, they will automatically take the place of the AI player. Others do not mind having Bots on their squad, but usually they are a definite disadvantage, as the enemy squad will normally exploit the Bot's programmed weaknesses, and will now make the Bot (or Bots) their primary target.

However, if you know that this is so, as you would with the noob or point player, you can watch the Bot's back, and anticipate the attacks on them. Bots do not have the ability to "lead" anyone, and will therefore never be on point. They are typically programmed to follow the *last* human player, and also to *immediately* assist any player in distress, human or Bot. Since they are run by the game code and software, they do have uncanny "aiming" ability, and will often dispatch enemies with an instant kill shot.

They also seem to have an ability to see through walls, and to know where enemy players are, before the human players do. These are their strengths, and they can be valuable team assets *if used properly*.

On a squad with two human players and two Bots, for example, the human players should stick closely together—they should never be more than 10 or 20 feet apart, and should basically function as "co-points" for the squad. Both Bots will follow the points closely, and will immediately aid them if needed. They will also "spot" enemies for you, and quickly kill them if they are in weapons range. Remember that they will be targeted as "weak points" on your squad, and defend them accordingly. Do not let them be cut off from the human players by obstacles or hazards like fire, or acid.

•They are programmed to avoid taking damage, even if it means lagging back for valuable seconds and being completely destroyed by the enemy•

A human player might choose to take a small amount of damage by running through a fire or hazard in order to not be left behind by their squad, but remember that a Bot will *not*. Bots will also heal or resupply you, even if they are critically injured, so remember to keep them healthy, especially if they have used their kit or supplies on another (human) player.

Bots typically will not use throwable or "settable" items, like grenades, bombs, or explosives, although they may pick them up and carry them. You can also give Bots health upgrades, but they will typically use them immediately, whether or not they actually "need" to at the time. Keep this in mind—watch them constantly, using your highly-developed sense of *situational awareness* to make sure that they are healthy and well-supplied with ammo.

Leading a squad with one or more Bot players is challenging, but it is a valuable tool for developing your skill as a gamer, and for understanding the mechanics of the game. If you understand their "thought" process and programming, it is possible or even easy to win rounds with them. If you do not, most likely you will be quickly destroyed by attrition, starting with the Bot players.

•The primary and critical mistake most often made by players who do not understand Bot coding and behavior is the tendency to "lag back" with the Bots•

Thus they become separated from the point player. This will cause the enemy to focus their attacks on the isolated human point, and will cause confusion among the Bots, as they will act "undecided" about whether to stay with the lagging human player, or to help the endangered human point.

Remember that they will not lead a squad, and will not "pass by" a human player to do so, since they are programmed to follow the last human player. If that is you, you should already be very close to the other human player or players, as explained above. If you follow this strategy, your Bots will become strong assets for the squad, rather than "weak links."

I have led a squad of three Bots against another squad of one human player and three Bots more than a few times, and the opposing player usually ends up quitting in disgust, because of how thoroughly they are being owned. Why does this happen? Because I understand the behavior and coding of both the Bots on my squad, *and* on the enemy team.

▪In other words, Bots are only as strong as the *weakest* human player—if that player is strong, they will be too▪

The take-away from this is that you *never* want that weakest player to be *you*.

▪Vote Kicks and Bans▪

Many if not most game servers will the option available through the menu to "kick," or "ban" someone. If so, it will usually only apply to a member of your own team or squad, obviously so that a pro player from the winning team cannot be kicked by disgruntled "pwnees." You may also be kicked by the "admin" (administrator) of a particular server, usually for violating a server rule that you may or may not be aware of.

▪Kicks are temporary, and you can typically rejoin the server immediately if you like▪

A ban, on the other hand, may be "temporary," or "*permanent.*" Remember that most game servers are privately owned and administered, and that you are a "guest" of the server and its host. Therefore you should conduct yourself as you would in someone's home. If you are spilling drinks and breaking furniture, you would expect to be thrown out and not invited back, correct? If you are banned, you can request that the ban be lifted if you visit the host's website and state your case, but usually this is a waste of time, unless you are especially contrite.

Some servers are run by immature gamers, and you may be banned for having too much skill, or not enough. You may be banned for a good reason, or for no reason. Either way, get over it, move on, and don't take it personally. Learn from the experience, and be more careful about your behavior in the future.

You may find yourself on either side of this issue. Sometimes you will join a server and will be immediately kicked without explanation. As confusing and hurtful as this may be, usually it happens because the other players are waiting for a friend to join, and are "saving their seat" so to say. Polite folks will tell you as much, and *ask* you to leave, and when they do, it is always best to do so, because if you don't, they will kick you anyway, and why would you want to be a part of a team that does not want you?

If you are kicked by an admin, it may be to make room for another player, or because you have an offensive "handle." If this happens, a message will usually appear telling you so, and why the kick happened. Some servers will "auto-kick" you for "team-killing" too often, or for having too high of a ping. Don't take this personally—accidents happen, and if you do team-kill someone inadvertently, it is always a good idea to immediately (and publically) apologize so that no one thinks you are doing it on purpose.

If your ping sucks, you will have a lot of lag, and you may want to look for another server with less latency anyway, so getting kicked earlier rather than leaving in disgust later is probably better for you and your confidence level.

Smaller teams or squads may look at your game profile and determine that you do not have enough "experience" or "hours" to suit them, and will kick you based on those criteria, again usually without saying a word. **You can prevent this from happening by setting your game profile to** "private," so that only your skill (or lack thereof) can be used to determine your "newness."

Some players with only a few hours in a specific game may have hundreds or thousands of hours of gaming experience in others, and a highly developed sense of *situational awareness*. This player would be a valuable asset regardless of how many or how few "game hours" they had.

For this reason, I never look at profiles when trying to determine whether to vote kick or ban someone. I look at their skill level, attitude, and willingness to help the team.

▪Rage and Grief▪

Related to the topic of kicks and bans is the subject of rage and grief. "Rage" usually occurs as a result of being owned, and it typically refers not only to the emotion of intense anger, but also to the immediate exiting of the server in disgust. This would be called "raging," or "rage quitting." If you find yourself becoming enraged, (and it happens to almost all gamers, at least once in a while) think about why this is happening.

▪Usually it is the result of *tunnel vision*, destroyed confidence, and disappointment with the *self*, rather than with the team or the squad▪

If this happens to you, before you rage, try to re-focus yourself by changing roles or tactics within the game, or ask your team or squad for extra help or protection.

An even uglier side of rage is "grief," or "griefing."

This is when the enraged player decides to either self-destruct, or to destroy their own team, since they believe that they have been wronged or let down by them somehow. If you see or notice a player turning their weapons on themself or on their own team, you should initiate a kick or ban vote *sooner* rather than later, because if you wait too long, or long enough for everyone else to notice, it may be too late for your team to recover from the damage the griefer has caused. This may cost you an entire round, or the entire battle, and this is what the griefer is hoping to accomplish.

Simply start the kick vote from the options menu or console, and type in general chat "(player name) is griefing, vote kick please." This will alert everyone else to their actions, and explain why you are attempting to kick them. Most folks do not want griefers around for one second longer than necessary, and will quickly vote to kick.

▪Resist the urge to grief your team or a particular player, no matter how much you think they deserve it▪

There is absolutely *nothing* to gain by griefing. You will not make any friends, people will remember what you have done, and you will probably end up raging anyway. A better strategy would be to tell your team why you are upset, and at whom, and if justified, to ask for a kick vote against that player, or a change in strategy.

If neither is forthcoming, then simply and quietly type "gga," (good game all) and leave for greener pastures and a better team.

You and everyone else will be better off.

▪Map Selection▪

Every game will offer a selection of "maps" or "boards" on which the battles will take place. There may be ten or more different ones to choose from, and some games even allow players to upload their own "modded" (custom made) maps. Maps are designed to challenge the players, and some are better suited for a particular player type, style, or vehicle, than are others.

Since I am primarily a tanker, I tend to favor larger maps, with areas of open ground, versus "urban" maps filled with buildings and

obstructions. You may prefer urban areas filled with house to house, "mano-a-mano" melee combat. Many gamers have such preferences, and tend to "specialize" in a particular player type, vehicle, or map. There is nothing inherently "wrong" with this point of view, other than you are limiting your enjoyment of the game, and your achievements within it, by always doing the same things, in the same place, with the same player type.

▪Even pro players are generally highly specialized, in that you will usually not find them outside of the "box" they have constructed for themselves▪

The take-away from this is that if you already know for a fact that you prefer a certain type of map, then stick with that type, and develop a high degree of expertise within it. Every map has certain spots or areas that are "sweet" for each particular player type, and some have more than others. For example, Snipers will look for areas that offer both concealment and access to a large field of view.

Assaults will want access to equipment and team assets, and will locate in areas that can be covered by air and land vehicles, like choppers and tanks. Medics will follow Assaults, and Engineers will normally flank and precede them, to mine roads, repair vehicles, provide cover, and destroy enemy assets.

Therefore an Engineer will normally avoid maps with few or no uses for heavy weapons and tactics—you don't use a bazooka to swat flies, for example. Likewise, a Medic is practically useless on a map filled with Snipers, because they will not be located closely enough to support, and moving between them will normally make *you* the focus of the enemy Snipers, as well as revealing your own team's positions.

However:

▪I would encourage every gamer who *really* wants to expand their skills, and *truly* challenge themselves, to venture into maps and player types that are *not* familiar to them▪

Yes, you will get owned a lot, but you will also *learn* a lot. If you want to *know* the enemy, *become* the enemy. If Snipers are your bane, your "Achilles heel," then learn to snipe. If you think like a Sniper, and act like one, you will be two steps ahead of the enemy. Likewise with Engineers. If you carry mines and heavy weapons, and deploy and use them, you will learn the best places on each map to do so, and the weakest areas to attack on enemy vehicles— their "soft spots" if you will.

This will help you learn to protect those same areas on your own vehicles, and avoid traps and mines, because you will look at an area, and your sense of *situational awareness* will tell you that a certain spot is where you are most likely to be attacked, and with what weapon. This is particularly useful with squad-based games, regardless of what map you are on.

▪Spawn Point Selection▪

Depending on the type of game you are playing, you may have the ability to "re-spawn" within the same round. After a given number of seconds, usually from 10 to 30, you will have another "life" to lose on the battlefield. Spawn point selection will be crucial at this point, because if you spawn in at the right place, you can change the game and help win battles for your team. The "proper" spawn point is constantly changing, and will be heavily dependent on your sense of *situational awareness*.

Normally you will be able to spawn at any waypoint held by your team, or in the process of being captured by them. If you are part of a squad, you can typically spawn in wherever one of your squad mates is currently located, or where the squad leader is. In some games, a "beacon" can be placed by the leader, and then all members can repeatedly spawn at that location until the beacon is destroyed by the enemy.

▪Timing is crucial when selecting the proper spawn point, therefore if an objective is about to be captured (or lost) that may be your clue to provide reinforcements▪

If your squad is capturing a waypoint, you may be able to pick up some quick and easy points by spawning in at just the right moment before the capture—even if you are only there for *one second*, you will still get the points. The same principle applies to the *defense* of a waypoint. Helping your team or squad prevent the loss of a crucial objective will go a long way towards achieving victory.

In some squad-based games, there are no "fixed" spawn points—you can do so anywhere that is out of the line of sight of the opposing team, so again, choose your location wisely. For maximum effectiveness, plan and coordinate your re-spawns with your squad. Spawn in together, and attack together.

▪Resist the urge to "noob rush" your re-spawn before your team or squad is ready▪

If you spawn in at the "wrong" place or time, you may be helping to lose the round for your team, or even worse—you may be subjected to "spawn rape."

"Raping" a spawn point is a terrible habit practiced by the most immature and mediocre players you will find. They will situate themselves at or near known spawn points on each map, (usually in a tank or vehicle) and then repeatedly kill players within seconds of spawning. This awful and unsporting behavior is usually directed against the newest and most helpless players in the round—the noobs who are unable to defend themselves, and who lack the knowledge to quickly switch to another spawn point that is hopefully not being camped by such an abusive player.

Most servers have rules against this type of behavior, especially regarding the "main" or "uncap" base of the opposing team. If you are found there, you may be kicked or banned. If you are being spawn-raped, ask for an admin to assist you by removing the offending player. If one is available, they are usually quick to act to control these types of rule violations. If not, the best defense is to alert your team that it is happening, and then select another spawn point from the options menu. As a last resort, simply find another server where rule enforcement is a higher priority.

▪Leveling Up and Awards▪

Many games will offer awards and achievements for certain accomplishments. Developing proficiency with a certain weapon, for example, may "unlock" your access to another, more powerful weapon. Thus noobs are "penalized" in many games simply for being new, in that more experienced players will have more powerful and accurate weapons—the better to own you with. This means that you will want to develop a strategy that will allow you to quickly gain access to more skills and better weapons.

▪Usually this means fully developing a single player type at a time, rather than building up a little bit of each character▪

This is the process that tends to train players in a particular player type, in effect building the box in which they are confined. In other words, if you spend all your game hours as an Assault, you will soon have all the "bad-ass" weapons and mods that are available, whereas if you divide your game time between all player types, it may be weeks or months until you have all the "cool stuff" that each may carry.

Developing all four types a little at a time is probably the better strategy for the long-term, but it is a confidence-destroyer, in that you will be getting owned a lot as you do so. For this reason, you may wish to fully develop each player type in turn, starting with Medic, for example, because you will be able to heal yourself (and others) often, and you will need to do so, because you will be getting shot up a lot.

•The process of leveling up each player type will be the same•

Acquire a weapon or tool, then develop your proficiency with it, by actually using it to do stuff with. Even if you hate shotguns, for example, when you are awarded one, make sure to use it for a few hours, because doing so will typically gain you the "points" that you need to get the awesome assault rifle that you *really* want. The same can be said for each upgrade you receive, for each player type.

In general, joining a squad and working with them to achieve team objectives will quickly facilitate the process of leveling up, because not only will you gain experience through exposure to other player types and weapons, but you will usually receive double points for any objectives that you achieve. For example, healing a *team* member may award you 10 points, but healing a *squad* mate gets you 20.

The "big money" as far as points go will be found in getting certain "awards" such as the Gold Star for the round, or the "Medal of Achievement" for this or that. These medals and awards typically come with *thousands* of points, sometimes five thousand or more, so you can see how getting them helps you level up that much faster.

You can usually track your progress towards a certain award or achievement in the options menu, and you can also determine exactly what actions you need to take to obtain it. A "Combat Vehicle Efficiency Pin" for example, may come with 5000 points, and may require you to get 500 kills with a specific vehicle. It may also apply to several vehicles, so if you already have the award for one type, you may want to switch to another, so that you can get multiple awards of the same Pin.

Some players become fixated on earning every possible award, commendation, and honor that is possible to obtain within the game, and to them I say "Ooh rah!" but to me this is an unnecessary distraction from the actual playing of the game, and therefore my focus has never been to achieve *all* the possible awards, merely the ones that were necessary to gain access to a particular weapon or item. You may fall into either camp, but you should be aware of, and stay focused on, the acquisition of more and better weapons and *skills,* versus the number of medals on your "chest."

▪Kit Selection▪

Most games will offer you the ability to equip items prior to the start of each round, and these will vary for each player or character type. Your "Kit" holds all of the items and weapons that you will be able to access during a particular round or "life." Typically you will have a primary weapon, (like a rifle or shotgun) a secondary weapon, (like a pistol, knife, or other "melee" item) an ammunition or health supply, (or both) and perhaps an additional item like a throwable weapon, or a defibrillator.

Within a few seconds of their "death," you may also be able to "pick up" a fallen comrade or enemy's Kit, and thereby gain access to whatever equipment *they* are carrying. This is a terrific way to acquire and test out weapons and items that you have not "earned" yet. If you do, keep in mind that you will "lose" the gear at your next re-spawn. If you really want to make a friend, (and look like a pro gamer) pick up a fallen Medic's Kit and "revive" them with their own defibrillator. <u>It is one of *the* slickest moves a gamer can pull off</u>.

▪At the beginning of each round, or during a re-spawn, you will again be able to choose the items that you will carry, and it is definitely to your advantage to choose them wisely▪

Avoid complacency when choosing items for your Kit, and do not fall into the default trap, because much as it is unwise to bring a knife to a gunfight, it is equally stupid to bring a shotgun to a battlefield where you will engage the enemy from hundreds of yards away. If you do, you will be pointing what is essentially a big noisy stick in their direction. In this case, you might as well have an actual wooden stick and be yelling "Bang!" as you gesture towards the enemy, for all the damage you will be doing to them.

Conversely, that same shotgun will become an "pwner of n00bs" in an urban environment, as you move from room to room and house to house, "taking out the trash" as you go. An Engineer with a rocket or grenade launcher might as well have a baseball bat in this same situation, because if he fires his weapon in a room or hallway, he (and perhaps his whole squad) will be re-spawning somewhere else in about ten seconds.

▪Your choice of items will of course be limited to the those that you have "earned" and have access to, and these will typically be visible from the options menu▪

The obvious choices are the most powerful, accurate, and useful weapons and items that you have in your inventory, for each particular map or environment that you will be moving through, subject to the weapons and items that your squad or team is *already* carrying. Four rocket-launcher wielding troops may *look* intimidating, but as far as "effectiveness," I would be much more afraid of a squad with one rocket launcher, one machine gun, one assault rifle, and one shotgun.

In this case, knowing what weapons type the enemy is carrying will help you plan your attacks against them, because, as in the above example, engaging the squad of "tube noobs" in a hallway would mean certain death for them, if planned semi-coherently, because they cannot fire them without damaging each other, and they cannot fire more than one or two at once. Likewise, engaging a squad carrying nothing but shotguns would best be done at a range of 50 yards or more, perhaps with rifles or rockets.

In urban or close combat situations, a "melee" weapon is *invaluable,* for at least two good reasons:

•Firstly, it never runs out of ammo•

You can bash 100 zombie skulls with a bat, and the only "cost" will be a very wet bat. You might need hundreds or thousands of rounds of ammo to do the same damage with a rifle or shotgun.

•Secondly, melee weapons are relatively quiet•

Loud noises seem to attract the attention of other enemy soldiers, and perhaps even larger and more powerful monsters or zombies, so dispatching the occasional stray quickly and *quietly* with a melee weapon is often the preferred course of action. Plus, you may enjoy adding our friend Shankey McShank's dog tags to *your* collection as much as he enjoys adding yours to *his*.

The ability to equip a health supply or an ammo cache to heal and re-supply your squad is also very useful—even better if one member carries health, and one ammo. Four members carrying ammo supplies means lots of bullets for everyone, but does nothing to plug any leaky holes they may suddenly develop. Likewise, four squad mates carrying health kits means that they will all have red rosy cheeks—right up until the moment they are killed after they run out of ammo.

•Mentoring or Shadowing•

One very valuable training technique I have used (and highly recommend) is the practice of "shadowing" a pro player. You can do this with or without their knowledge and consent, but you are probably better off asking them if you can "tag along" with them. You may even offer to heal, re-supply, or repair for them.

Step one in this process would be identifying the pros on your team, and you can easily determine this by checking the stats board. Anyone in the top five is obviously doing something right, so look for one that is spawning as the player type you prefer, or is using your weapon or vehicle of choice. You may also choose to shadow someone who is an expert with a weapon or vehicle that you are *not* familiar with, but would like to be.

Ideally, you would join their squad, and take up a position very nearby—become their "right hand-man." Be very careful that you do not "cramp their style," or interfere with their game or stats in any way, by "stealing" their kills, or by revealing their position to the enemy, for example. Those actions will not make you any friends. However, if you do want to make a friend of the pro you are shadowing, <u>take ridiculous risks to help them</u>.

▪Charge up under heavy fire to revive or re-supply them, or to repair their damaged vehicle▪

They will be impressed by your "courage," and may even send you a "friend request" so they can invite you to game with them again. I have made friends of many pro gamers (and learned a *lot*) by doing just that—acting as the "Corpsman" for a pro squad, and doing pretty much nothing but heal and revive them. My stats were terrible, but my intentions were good, and people noticed me.

They invited me to their squads, said good things about me, and offered to teach me the "tips and tricks" that made them the pros that they were. Acting in such a support role will teach you humility, and will vastly improve your sense of *situational awareness,* as you focus intently on helping others, rather than yourself. You will *notice* when they are injured, or out of ammo, or about to be destroyed. You will learn to *anticipate* and respond to enemy attacks like a pro does, simply by watching them do it.

▪Ask them what they think you should do—then *do it*▪

If they say, "Stand over there, and watch for enemy tanks, and when you see one, say "Tank!"—then do that. If they say "Bring a rocket launcher on your next re-spawn, or an ammo supply," there is probably a good reason for them telling you that, and if you do it, you will find out what that reason is. Please do not ask for advice and then not take it, as you will become more of a hindrance than a help, and will most likely be kicked from the squad, or otherwise "left behind" to be quickly destroyed by the enemy.

One particularly good question to ask a pro is:

"What control mapping scheme do you use?" Or "Where should I map my (blank) key?"

Pro players are usually happy to tell you *where* they map a particular control, and *why* they do so. <u>This information is gold</u>, so pay attention to any and all advice you are given.

Once you have "shadowed" a pro player for a while, you might even ask them if they would "mentor" you. You could simply ask if you can add them to your friends list, or if they can show you how to use a particular weapon or vehicle.

▪Squading and mentoring with a pro gamer is a huge confidence-builder for you, because it will immediately boost your K/D ratio, if only because they will be protecting you from being owned▪

It will also be a burden for them, so be considerate and grateful if you do find willing mentors. Be sure to recognize the help that they give you, and to thank them for it.

▪Clans and Groups▪

Another invaluable source for acquiring skill and mentors will be to join a "Clan," or gaming group. You may ask to join such a group, or you may be asked to do so. It is an honor to be asked to join, of course, but you must be careful about doing so. Some groups and server hosts dislike each other, and will instantly kick or ban anyone who joins their server while displaying the "tags" of an opposing group. Clan members typically display their tag as part of their player name, as in {Clan Name} (Player Name), and "recruits" or "probationary" members may display a lower case "r" after the Clan name.

Clans and groups usually have a strict code of conduct for their members, so if you are unwilling or unable to follow that code, do *not* join that particular Clan. If you observe unsporting behavior from a clanner, or see one using a hack, for example, you can report them to their leaders by going to the Clan's website and posting your case there, along with your evidence. Most Clans will deal very harshly and quickly with *proven* misconduct by a member.

Gaming groups may require some form of monthly "dues" payment, but this usually guarantees you a reserved spot on their server, and they also will have regular "scrims" or matches with other groups. If you join a "pub" or public server, and see that the opposing team is made up entire of players with the same Clan tag, you can be sure that they are using voice comms, will be somewhat skilled, and are probably going to own you and your team.

However, it can be good experience for you anyway, and if they are impressed with your skill, they may invite you to join them, or you could ask for an invite.

I have been a member of a couple of Clans, <u>and I highly recommend them for anyone who wants to seriously develop their gaming skills</u>. "Multi-Clanning" by the way, is usually frowned upon, in that one Clan will not allow you to simultaneously be part of another, competing one—at least in the same "gaming universe." If they find out that you are, most likely *both* Clans will dismiss you—so don't do it. However, you *can* be a member of one Clan for one game, and another for a *different* game, and there is no dishonor or disloyalty in taking this path.

▪Pro Location▪

A more passive approach to *shadowing* would be to simply become aware of *where* the pros on your team are locating themselves during the round, and what they are doing when they get there. When I first starting playing wartime simulations, I noticed that the pros on the team tended to hang out together, <u>in certain places on the map</u>. They would take up a position, then immediately establish a perimeter, drop ammo and health supplies, and proceed to own the enemy.

▪All of this makes perfect sense, of course, and very closely resembles the actions of actual soldiers in combat situations▪

Why do they do this?

<u>Because it is a great strategy</u>. Locating and deploying an attack or defense force *properly* helps to ensure that everyone in the squad has ammo, and health, and that there are four pairs of "eyes on target" rather than one. Such a force in the right place, at the right time, can be a game-changer and battle-winner—and it often is, in "real life" and in the gaming universe.

If you are too shy to ask about joining a pro squad, or too much of a "Lone Wolf" to want to squad up just yet, you can simply locate yourself in close proximity. You don't have to "say" anything—just hang out. You *are* on the same team, after all, with the same objectives. Watch their backs, cover them when they advance, throw down ammo or health, be a good "battle-buddy," and you will make friends quickly.

▪You will also learn by "osmosis," as simply watching others do well, and how they do it, will be of great help to you in your quest to be an *pwner of n00bs*▪

◀AFTERWORD▶

In the sport of online gaming, the obvious difference between "pwner" and "pwnee" is the level of skill that each brings to the battlefield. Skill can take hundreds or thousands of hours to build and develop, or it can take only a few dozen.

As with most things in life, a good attitude and a willingness to *listen* will take you far. This guide is filled with useful information that if studied and applied will quickly flatten out your learning curve, such that no matter what game you play, and what character or player type you choose, you will stride across battlefields as a confident warrior, not cower fearfully as an anxious n00b.

▪Remember these important strategies for gaming success▪

Your hardware settings will be optimized and properly configured. Your controls will be properly mapped for perfect and easy access. Your weapons will stay hot, because you will *not* run out of ammo. Your K/D ratio will be high, because you will *always* have a highly-developed sense of *situational awareness,* and you will *never* display *tunnel vision.*

You will study and understand the mechanics of each game you play, and the AI coding of the Bots within them. You will use the tools of the game to help you succeed, rather than allowing the enemy to dominate you with them. The enemy will *never* surprise you, because you will see, hear, and kill them—before they do the same to you.

You will always spend a few hours in single-player mode before you go multi-player, and you will ensure that your video and audio options are optimized for ideal gaming performance *before* you go multi-player.

If you enjoyed reading *Pwning N00bs*, and you have benefitted from it, tell your friends! Your opinion counts, so feel free to leave a fair and honest review of my work on Amazon.

For information about other books by John David, including *Ten Questions – The Insider's Guide to Saving Money on Auto Insurance,* and the *Essays for the 99%,* visit my website: johndavidauthor.com.

◀KEY CONCEPTS▶

The Good, the Bad, and the Ugly

This chapter contains key concepts and utilities that have been referenced throughout the text. In the *ebook* version, useful (and free) programs are explained here and externally hyperlinked. Important concepts are hyperlinked back to the section of the text that explains them. Page numbers are provided in the paperback version.

▪The Good▪

•Programs and Utilities•

◄CPUID►

This is a free program that is very useful for determining what hardware you have in your system now, and what effect any changes or tweaks you make will have on that hardware. It is particularly useful when *overclocking*. CPUID is available as a free download, and it displays detailed information about your system in several categories, beginning with the CPU, as you might suspect. It will tell you what type of processor you have now, what speed it runs at, and what socket type it is.

It will also display the clock rate and FSB for the current settings you have, as well as the "cache" you have available.

CPUID also displays information about your "mainboard" (motherboard) and *bios*, and will show you the manufacturer, model, and chipset. The current *bios* information will help you determine if you need to "flash" or update it, as sometimes a simple update to the *bios* can make a significant difference in how your board performs. If your *bios* version is several years old, you may want to go to the manufacturer's website and look under the "support" category to see if an update is available. If so, be sure to follow the "flashing" instructions exactly, because if you don't, you may damage or render your motherboard inoperable.

The next tab displays your system's memory information—what brand, size, type, and speed you have. It will also show you the "clock rate," and "timings" that your memory is running at, as well as the "FSB:DRAM" ratio, **which is probably the most significant factor to know about your RAM.**

A 1:1 ratio here is considered the ideal, and the *easiest* way to achieve this is by using your mainboard's "auto-configure" setting, whereby it will adjust your timings automatically. If you prefer to set them manually, you will want to do an online search for your specific memory brand and type, then look for "timings" or "settings," and perhaps even "overclocking." **Adjusting and overclocking system memory is very complicated, and is not something that a beginner should take on.** It can be hazardous to your RAM, like all overclocking, in that the particular component may be damaged or destroyed in the process.

A "graphics" tab is also included, and here you will discover information about your GPU or GPUs—again what brand, type, and speed, and what your current clock settings are.

▪CPUID is an invaluable resource for the PC gamer and system builder▪

You will be able to discover more crucial information about your current hardware setup in five minutes, without ever opening your case, than you would in an hour or two with your hands inside the case. Before you do *anything* to your system, use this program to determine your "baseline" information, and take careful notes about everything you see. You may even want to place a "system specs" file on your desktop, for easy reference later. If you are considering a CPU upgrade, be sure to use this program before you do so.

◄FRAPS►

This is another extremely useful and free program that can be used to show your current video display rate of frames per second, or FPS. It is a very low impact program, and you can set the numerical display to show in the location of your choice, typically in one corner of your screen. Run it during each gaming session while you are initially tweaking your settings.

▪Watch for particular places or situations where the frame rate drops substantially below 30 FPS▪

Make your settings adjustments based on your visual preferences, with the goal of "evening out" the entire gaming session at a *minimum* of 30 FPS or better. Some tweaks, like turning "AA" off for example, may have a very large impact on frame rate. Others may have little or none.

Another very useful application of FRAPS is that you can also record screen shots of your awesome accomplishments—or questionable actions by other players, such as those you suspect of hacking.

Simply "ghost" the player in question, then start recording. Video evidence of aim, wall, or speed hacks is golden, and if you submit it to the server or game host, may even result in the permanent ban of the "gamer." Make sure to grab their "player ID" as well, from the console, because the in-game video will only show their current player "handle," not their registered game ID. Simply mentioning that you are recording what you believe is a hack or exploit is often enough to induce the player in question to immediately drop from the server, especially if you mention FRAPS.

You can download the program from the website, and you must be sure to open and run it each time you want to use it, or set it to start automatically with *Windows*. You do *not* want to be "in game," discover that you need to know your frame rate, or record something, then realize that you must now exit the game to start the program. From the "settings" tab, you can also configure the color to display the FPS indicator, the location to store saved screen shots and videos, and the particular key or keys to take the screenshot or start recording video. As with any other control key, you want to map these carefully, so that you will actually be able to remember and use them, when needed.

Make sure to set the quality level for recording video, but remember that higher quality will take more hard drive space. Keep in mind that recording real-time video also puts demand on your system, and depending on the strength of that system, this "drag" could be a "game-changer" (and loser) for you. Recording video also takes *huge* amounts of space on your hard drive, (depending on the quality settings you choose) perhaps as much as a gigabyte of space per minute, or more.

◄TEAMSPEAK►

This is a commonly used VOIP (Voice Over Internet Protocol) program. Many game servers will also host a teamspeak server in conjunction with the game. The program is free to download and to use, but for each game and server you will need the server IP address and a password to access it. This information is usually posted on the server banner when you join.

▪The teamspeak server will typically have "rooms" for each side of the battle, one for your team, and one for the enemy, for example▪

Obviously you do not want everyone on the same channel, as this would negate the usefulness of voice communication in developing strategy and tactics, because if the enemy can hear exactly what the plan is, there will be no element of surprise. There may also be other "rooms" on the comms server for "Admins" or "Chat" or what have you. Just make sure that you are in the correct room for the team (and perhaps squad) that you are on.

Some games will have VOIP ability already built into the game code, and you may prefer to use the in-game service. Many gamers believe that the in-game chat causes extra latency, or lag, and therefore prefer to use a third party program. The server host may manipulate the in-game chat code as well, so that one team hears *all* the voice chat, but the other hears only their own team. This is an obvious advantage for one side over the other.

◀NOTES▶

www.ingramcontent.com/pod-product-compliance
Lightning Source LLC
Chambersburg PA
CBHW081310170526
45166CB00011B/3472